Planning

·your·

Wedding

PLANNING
· YOUR ·
WEDDING

Joyce Robins

CHANCELLOR

PRESS

First published as *Hamlyn Help Yourself Guide: Planning Your Wedding* in 1989 by Reed Consumer Books Limited

This edition published in 1993 by Chancellor Press
an imprint of Reed Consumer Books Limited
Michelin House, 81 Fulham Road, London SW3 6RB
and Auckland, Melbourne, Singapore and Toronto

ISBN 1 85152 368 5

A CIP catalogue record for this book is available from
the British Library

Printed in Great Britain

Contents

Introduction

In every century, in widely differing cultures, marriage has been held to be one of life's most important events; hence the extent of the ceremony and tradition attached to the wedding day. The various elements of wedding pageantry – the ring, the cake, the bouquets – may have their origins in ancient fertility symbols and customs long forgotten but they all contribute to creating a very special atmosphere, a memory to last a lifetime.

No couple today is likely to follow custom slavishly, but while some prefer to throw it all aside and do their own thing, many more find that weddings bring out the tradition-loving side of their nature. They feel that the ceremonious dignity of wedding etiquette enhances the occasion and get pleasure from knowing that they are following in the footsteps of millions of happy couples before them.

The rules of 'who does what' have relaxed a good deal over the last two decades, and the days when the wedding preparations were entirely the province of the bride and her mother, with the bridegroom standing patiently on the sidelines and the bride's father waiting with an open cheque book, are long gone. Couples are now more likely to plan together and share expenses but most still find that their family's hopes and wishes still play an important part in shaping their decisions.

Whether your wedding is large or small, formal or informal, shared by two dozen people or two hundred, there are many alternatives to consider, many possibilities to discuss. There is no blueprint for a successful wedding, but knowing all the options can help you to make the choices that are right for you.

1

The Engagement

Engagements no longer have any legal basis but most couples still regard them as a serious commitment, as a public announcement of their intention of sharing their lives permanently. Few of today's brides-to-be are set a-flutter by a sudden and unexpected proposal. Unless they are caught up in a whirlwind courtship, for most couples, the decision to marry usually comes out of a tacit understanding and both partners will have already given much thought to the implications. All the same, the engagement period, as well as being a happy, exciting time, also presents the couple with an opportunity to consider their relationship in a new light, talk through their attitudes to money, sex, children and work and face up to the joys and the problems their life together may bring.

You may think that deciding to marry is your own private business but as soon as you make your decision public, other people become involved. Mothers may be planning the guest list before the ring is on your finger; relatives want to know when the announcement is to appear in the paper so that they can send it to yet more relatives you hardly knew you had; friends want to know the date, the church, the honeymoon destination, even the colour of the bouquets.

Some couples prefer to avoid the whole business by buying a licence and marrying a couple of days after the decision is taken but most enjoy the good wishes and the feeling of being the centre of attention for at least a short time. Long engagements are not usual these days, unless, for example, one or other partner has to leave for a tour of duty overseas, or the couple are still in the middle of their studies at colleges in different parts of the country. Then an engagement is their way of saying that they have made their final decision, even though circumstances mean that the wedding has to wait a while.

Most engagements last for a few months, just long enough to make all the wedding arrangements, but there is no set pattern. Couples who have been living together for years may announce their engagement and then go on to observe all the conventions of rings, announcements and parties.

Breaking the news

Few young men today expect to ask permission from a girl's father and give an account of their future prospects – unless, of course, the couple are under eighteen, in which case by law they need parental consent to marry. All the same, parents are just as concerned about the future happiness of their offspring as ever they were, so a few quiet words with parents on both sides before broadcasting your news to the world will reassure anxious mothers and over-protective fathers and set the scene for a happier relationship all round.

Convention says that the bride's parents should be told first – certainly this is only common courtesy if you are expecting them to pay all or part of the wedding costs – then the groom's parents. Even if you are not close to your parents and have lived away for years, it is only polite to tell them the news before 'outsiders'. After that come relatives and close friends.

Whether you choose to write or telephone with the good news, try to make all the calls or send all the letters at roughly the same time so that there is no risk of Aunt Agatha ringing Aunt Olga to say, 'Isn't it wonderful about dear Christabel', only to have Aunt Olga saying, '*What* about Christabel?' It is easy to overlook someone in the first flurry of excitement, so avoid mistakes by making a list of everyone who needs to be told and ticking them off, one by one.

If your family has an aunt who has not spoken to her sister for years or a 'black sheep' who once did something shady and has not been seen at a family gathering since, this could be the time to heal a rift. A brief note telling your news is sufficient, without making any reference to past troubles. If your letter is ignored, then you will have one less person to worry about when you make your guest list!

Announcing the engagement

You might want to announce your engagement in *The Times* or the *Daily Telegraph* because it is 'the thing' to do, or put an announcement in the local paper to spread the word. This is useful if you have a large circle of friends and acquaintances or if you live away from your home town and would like ex-colleagues or old school friends to hear the news. Make sure, before announcing your engagement in the press, that relatives and close friends have been told. They should not have to read the news for the first time in the paper.

Formal newspaper announcements read as follows:
Mr R.W. Black and Miss A.S. White
The engagement is announced between Roger Winston,
son of Mr and Mrs Cyril Black of Birmingham, and
Amy Samantha, daughter of Mr and Mrs Herbert White
of The Brambles, Twitterton, West Sussex.

or

Mr and Mrs Herbert White are pleased to announce
the engagement of their only daughter Amy
to Mr Roger Black, son of Mr and Mrs Cyril Black of Birmingham.

When the parents on either side are divorced, or one of them has died, it is usual to make this clear in the wording: for instance, 'daughter of Mr Herbert White of Twitterton, West Sussex and Mrs Iris White of Liverpool' or 'son of Mr Cyril Black of Birmingham and the late Mrs Edna Black'. Even if the bride's mother has re-married and emigrated, her name should appear in the announcement: 'daughter of Mr Herbert White of Twitterton, West Sussex, and Mrs Iris Munroe of Kingston, Jamaica'.

If the wedding date has already been set, the announcement might say 'The engagement is announced and the wedding will shortly take place between . . . ' A more formal version of the announcement might be:

Herbert and Araminta White are happy to announce
the engagement of their daughter Amy to Roger,
son of Cyril and Dora Black of Birmingham.

Professional titles and military ranks are always included, for instance 'Lt Roger Black, son of Mr and Mrs Cyril Black of Birmingham and Amy . . .'

The engagement party

An engagement party may be held to announce the good news, or simply to celebrate. Either way, it should be held as soon as possible, as the occasion will lose some of its excitement if everyone has already given their congratulations and made their wedding jokes on other occasions. The party can be as small and intimate or as large and as glossy as you like.

If you are following tradition, then the bride's parents arrange (and pay for) the party at their home and her mother issues the invitations. The guests might be immediate family only – perhaps just parents, siblings and grandparents – or the entire family down to the last second cousin twice removed, or a mixture of friends and family. If the couple are giving their own party, especially if they live away from home, they might invite only friends on both sides. Tact is needed if you decide to be selective and ask just a few relatives and friends. When Uncle Clarence finds that he has been left off the guest list, he is unlikely to appreciate the fact that you *like* Uncle Charlie better.

There is no need to send printed cards; an invitation by word of mouth or a simple note is sufficient and, if you are not holding the party at home, it can be a few drinks in the pub after work, a meal at a top-flight restaurant, a picnic on the river-bank – or anything else that appeals to you. You may decide to miss out speeches altogether but if you include them, they usually take the form of the bride's father (or uncle or old family friend) announcing the engagement, if most of the guests have not already heard the news, and wishing the couple health and happiness, then the groom proposing the health of both sets of parents. When the party includes a sit-down meal, the bride sits on the groom's left with her parents next to her; the groom's mother sits on his right with her husband next to her.

There are no hard and fast rules about whether or not to ask a divorced parent, who has perhaps married again, to the engagement party. It depends entirely on the relationships within the family, but if the party takes place in the family home, which either mother or father has left at some time in the past, their presence will usually be straining tolerance a little too far. In circumstances like this, it is often more tactful if the couple celebrate with each 'set' of parents separately.

Engagement presents are not usual, though some members of the family might like to give something to mark the occasion. A popular American custom, sometimes followed in Britain, is the 'shower party'. This is usually organized by friends of the bride and held in one of their homes. Showers are strictly female occasions and can be useful if, for instance, the bride is working away from home and her colleagues will not be at the wedding but feel they would like to mark the occasion. Each guest brings a small present for the bride's new home, fitting in with the theme of the shower: at a kitchen shower presents could be an egg whisk, a cake tin, ice cream scoop or something similar; at a linen shower presents might be tea-towels, pillowcases, a tablecloth or napkins. An alternative is a 'blue' or 'brown and orange' shower, but this is only really successful when friends are sure about the colour scheme of the girl's future home. A stack of blue presents would not be a delight to a girl who has set her heart on green and cream.

Engagement rings

Engagement rings are a very old custom; as early as Roman times the ring was an important part of the marriage contract. They have always been worn on the fourth finger of the left hand because the ancients believed that a vein in that finger ran directly to the heart.

There are no hard and fast rules on engagement rings. They may be bought as an investment or have no value other than sentiment; they can be handed down in the family or bought new in the high street. Many couples choose 'antique' rings, because this gives the opportunity of buying a better ring at a lower price.

There was a time when a hopeful young man would buy the ring, then present it to the girl if and when she accepted his proposal. Nowadays, most couples would expect to choose the ring together. Before the great shopping expedition, it is a good idea to discuss how much you want to pay, so that you can tell the sales assistant in advance, and not run the risk of falling in love with something well outside your price range and having to make do with 'second best'.

Problems can arise when there is a 'family ring' handed down from bride to bride in the bridegroom's family. It is never a good idea to present such a ring without talking it over first. Grandmother's heirloom, however handsome, may not be the style of ring a modern girl wants to wear every day and, anyway, many girls have a very definite idea of the type of engagement ring they want. A compromise might be to give the family ring as a separate present which might be worn occcasionally at family get-togethers.

Diamonds have been the front runners among precious stones since the nineteenth century, but they are expensive and there are plenty of attractive alternatives among the precious and semi-precious stones. Stones have a language of their own, and the girl's birthstone, carrying its own special meaning, has always been a popular choice:

January:	garnet, the symbol of truth
February:	amethyst, signifying sincerity
March:	aquamarine, meaning courage
April:	diamond for innocence
May:	emerald for success in love
June:	pearl for health and good looks
July:	ruby for contentment
August:	sardonyx, ensuring marital happiness
September:	sapphire, signifying wisdom
October:	opal for hope
November:	topaz, ensuring fidelity
December:	turquoise, bringing prosperity

It may be sensible to choose both engagement and wedding rings at the same time, so that they fit and look well together. Gold is measured in carats: the higher the carats, the purer the gold. However, the purer the gold the softer it is, so make sure your engagement and wedding rings are the same 'caratage' or the higher carat ring will suffer from constant contact with the other. You might consider buying companion rings, an engagement and a wedding ring specially designed to be worn on the same finger, possibly even fitting together.

Of course, you may prefer to ignore engagement rings altogether and put the money towards your honeymoon or your future home instead. Some girls wear the wedding ring on the fourth finger of the right hand, then transfer it to the left hand during the ceremony.

Getting to know the in-laws

The dragon mother-in-law may still be the butt of comedians' jokes but, in reality, most mothers are just as anxious as their future daughters- or sons-in-law to make the relationship work. If the family is a close one, however, it can be difficult accepting a virtual stranger as one of the inner circle, so both sides need to exercise a little caution in the early stages. You may see the world and marriage from completely different standpoints but it is often more tactful to keep your views to yourselves; no one is likely to change their way of life because you are out of sympathy with it.

There is no rule that you have to love your in-laws, or even like them, but if you can get along together without resentment or argument, life will be a great deal easier. It is easy enough to say that you are marrying the man, not his mother, but she is an important part of his life and the ties of affection and loyalty may be stronger than either of you realize. Keep your criticisms of your future in-laws to yourself; your partner is probably only too aware of their failings but may feel forced into defending them.

Deciding what to call your in-laws can be so tricky that many husbands and wives solve the problem by not using any name at all. However, there might come a time when you regret it. Most in-laws would appreciate the direct approach: 'What would you like me to call you?' This might open the way for a talk about the hesitations you both feel about the in-law relationship and clear the air on a number of minor problems.

No one expects the two sets of parents to accept one another as bosom friends, simply because their offspring have married. It is a good idea for the two sides to meet at least once before the wedding, and on this occasion it is the groom's mother who acts as hostess. If they are to meet for the first time on the day, then the groom's mother might ring or write to the bride's family beforehand, simply saying how pleased they are and how much they are looking forward to the wedding.

Broken engagements

Broken engagements are a fact of life and the future of the engagement ring is always a thorny subject. The rules of etiquette say that if the girl breaks off the engagement, she should return the ring. If her fiancé breaks things off, she is entitled to keep it – unless, of course, it is a family heirloom. In practice things usually sort themselves out according to circumstances: the ring may be the last thing the girl wants on her finger to remind her of a failed relationship, or in a 'no hard feelings' situation, it may be a pleasing keepsake.

Any valuable presents given from one to the other should be returned – or at least the offer should be made. The same applies to any engagement or wedding presents received from friends or relatives.

If the engagement was announced in the newspapers, the girl's family may insert a brief announcement

> The marriage between Roger Black and Amy White
> will not now take place.

If the invitations have already gone out, it is up to the girl's family, or the girl herself, to cancel them. Formal invitations should be cancelled in similarly formal language, for instance:

> Mr and Mrs Horace White announce that the marriage
> of their daughter Amy to Mr Roger Black will not
> now take place.

Before 1971 it was possible to sue for breach of promise if one party broke off an engagement. Now it is not possible to claim compensation for hurt feelings, or for money already spent on invitations or material for the dresses. However, the couple can resort to law if they cannot agree on a fair division of any property they may have bought jointly.

Wedding superstitions

Weddings have always been surrounded by superstition. Of course, not many of us admit to believing a word of it, but plenty of brides still go to the altar wearing 'something old, something new, something borrowed, something blue'. If you want to turn superstitious, just in case, there are several old beliefs and rhymes to help you plan your wedding with certain future happiness in mind.

To begin with, you need to choose the right month. One of the oldest sayings is 'Marry in May, rue the day' but other summer brides are supposed to be much more fortunate: 'Married during the month of June, life will be one long honeymoon' or 'Married in August's heat and drowse, lover and friend in your chosen spouse'. January brides risk losing their husbands early and the changeable nature of April means that couples married then will have plenty of ups and downs. The autumn and winter months seem quite a propitious time for marriage:

> Marry in September's shine,
> Your living will be rich and fine.
> If in October you do marry,
> Love will come but riches tarry.
> If you wed in bleak November,
> Only joy will come; remember
> When December's showers fall fast,
> Marry and true love will last.

Traditionally, certain days of the year were unlucky, particularly 11 February, 2 June, 2 November, 1 December, 28 December. There is advice, too, on the best day of the week, but as most brides marry on Saturday, they are obviously not taking it to heart:

> Monday for health
> Tuesday for wealth
> Wednesday, the best day of all
> Thursday for losses
> Friday for crosses
> Saturday, no luck at all.

The colour of your wedding day clothes is supposed to be another important issue:

White:	the *right* colour
Blue:	you can be sure your husband will be faithful
Yellow:	you will soon be ashamed of him
Grey:	your married life will include lots of travel
Pink:	you will soon become depressed
Black:	you will wish you were single again

Red and green are not considered suitable, and there is an argument over whether red or green is the 'unluckiest' wedding colour.

2

Making the Decisions

Some couples will have a clear idea of the type of wedding they want, even before the engagement is announced. Others will have to think through all the pros and cons of where to marry, where to hold the reception and how many people – not to mention which people – to ask. What matters most is making the choices that suit you, and this is not always as straightforward as it sounds when you are trying to consider the feelings of both families at the same time. Paying attention to details now will pay dividends in the smooth running of the wedding arrangements nearer the day.

Naming the day

Most couples marry on a Saturday, especially if they are planning a full-scale reception, as this is the day most of their friends will be free to join them. Though there is no legal bar to marrying on a Sunday, ministers are normally too busy with normal services to perform the ceremony.

As the Jewish sabbath is Saturday, Sunday is the popular day for Jewish weddings, and more and more register office weddings are taking place on Fridays. Register offices close on Saturday afternoons, so couples who prefer an evening reception find Friday afternoons a convenient time for the ceremony, so that their friends can join them after working hours.

June, Easter and Whitsun are still top of the list as wedding day choices. When marrying in March and September brought tax advantages, many 'beat the tax-man' weddings took place then, but the regulations have changed so that this no longer applies. Honeymoon plans may dictate the month you pick: November is not the best time for a Scottish lakeside idyll and July or August is likely to be far too hot for a Florida beach. You might also want to avoid the hay fever season, if either bride or groom normally suffers, or any time of year you usually suffer from minor ailments.

Before deciding on an exact date, check that the people you most want to be there will be free: that includes parents, your first choice for best man or bridesmaids and perhaps the relatives or friends who mean most to you.

At one time weddings had to take place, by law, before 3 p.m., and midday to 3 p.m. is still the most popular time as it enables guests travelling some distance to arrive punctually and get home again in the evening, and for the bride and groom to leave for their honeymoon destination. If your guests live nearby and you are not rushing from the reception to the airport, remember that it is usually one to one and a half hours after the time of the ceremony before any food is served, by which time bride and groom may be feeling weak at the knees and the guests may be hungry enough to eat the place mats. On the other hand, the bride's father may calculate that an afternoon reception will cut down on the drinks bill!

If economy is a prime consideration, an early wedding with drinks and snacks at around 11.30 a.m. can work well, but self-caterers often find late afternoon a better choice, so that they have all morning for last-minute preparations, then a couple of hours to rest before dressing for the ceremony.

Winter brides should bear in mind that the light will normally be poor by early afternoon, so if you want to pose outside the church door, the ceremony should take place before lunch-time. If you calculate that the weather may be too cold or wet for outdoor photography anyway, then you can arrange a suitable indoor setting for the formal poses and schedule the wedding for any time that suits you.

The wedding style

The wedding is primarily the bride and groom's day, so the choice of wedding style – large or small, religious or secular – must rest with them. However, most couples recognize that their families also have a big stake in 'the day' and many mothers have been looking forward for years to a white wedding for their only daughter. There can be no hard and fast rule: if there is disagreement, the final choice will depend on how close the family relationships are and how much the couple are willing to compromise to give their parents pleasure.

Church weddings

Church, chapel or synagogue will be the obvious choice for those with deeply held religious beliefs but many couples who never normally worship feel they want the solemnity, or the pageantry, of a religious ceremony. Others may be put off by the thought of all the trappings, the dozens of eyes trained on them, or the expense involved. This does not have to be the case: all you need for a church wedding is a bride and groom in ordinary street clothes and two witnesses. You can invite only close family members, or no one at all. No minister is likely to object if you want to forget about the trappings and concentrate on the religious significance of the service.

Register office weddings

Couples with no religious beliefs, or those who are divorced and unable, or unwilling, to re-marry in church, will marry with a simpler ceremony at a register office. This does not mean that the whole wedding has to be simple. You may not be able to ask as many people to attend the ceremony as in church – though some register offices can pack in several dozen – but you can still marry in full regalia and go on to the biggest, most elaborate reception you care to arrange.

Service of blessing

You may have seen Hollywood soap operas where the bride sweeps down the staircase of her own home towards the waiting minister, or marries in the midst of the rose garden, but this is not normally possible in the United Kingdom as marriages must take place in an officially registered building (see Chapter 3 for exceptions). If you long to celebrate your wedding in a place that has some special significance for you – the bluebell dell or a Cornish headland – ask your minister about a service of blessing. This is usually performed in church after couples have taken part in a civil ceremony, but some ministers are receptive to the idea of a romantic setting.

Double wedding

This can be arranged when two sisters or two brothers are planning to marry, but there is no reason why two friends should not marry in a double ceremony if their families are fairly close. A disadvantage may be the necessity to share the limelight on *the* day; on the other hand, some couples may enjoy the celebrations more if they are not the sole focus of attention. (See p.100 for procedure at double weddings.)

Seeing the minister

When you see the minister to arrange a date, he will probably want to know if you want the choir or bellringers as part of the ceremony, what music you would like and whether or not you would like him to give a short address. You may also talk about the order of service and the wording you want to use: for instance, do you want to include the word 'obey'? Remember to check on the scale of fees for organ, choir and so on. Jewish couples should discuss fees with the secretary to the synagogue.

It is a good idea to sound out the minister's views on tape-recording or videoing the ceremony, photographs in the church and confetti outside, and the flowers. If you want to have your own flower arrangements inside the church, check whether there are restrictions on size, colour or the placing of the arrangements – for instance, some ministers allow flowers on the altar, others do not. You may be able to join with other couples marrying on the same day to pay for the church decoration or liaise on colour schemes and placing with the person who is arranging flowers on the church's normal rota for the week.

If you have a minister in the family or among your friends you may want him to perform the ceremony and this should, of course, be discussed with the minister at the outset; there will normally be no problem. The same applies to arranging for a friend to play the organ, though it is usual to pay the regular organist anyway.

In some churches, ministers will want to instruct the couple in the religious significance of marriage and more formal instruction may be necessary if the couple belong to different denominations or faiths. Sometimes it is possible to arrange an interdenominational service but this is very much a matter for the clergymen involved and it is wise to consider whether such a service might offend many of the guests.

Seeing the registrar

When you notify the registrar of your intended marriage and book a date he will advise on residential qualifications and the legal papers you require. Ask about the fees, how long the ceremony will last, how many guests you are allowed and whether or not confetti is allowed. Remember to check if there is some reasonably attractive background for the photographs as you leave the office.

The guest list

However large your wedding, you will probably have to leave out *someone* with a distant claim to be there, so it is better to decide on the boundaries of the guest list right from the beginning. There are plenty of possibilities:
○ As many relatives, friends and colleagues as you can pack in
○ Family only, with all relatives on both sides invited
○ Close family only
○ All relatives and a few close friends
○ Close family and close friends only
○ Relatives only at the reception and a party for friends afterwards
○ Relatives, friends and colleagues invited to the church but a reception only for those you would normally invite to a party

There can be problems when the bride's parents are paying for the wedding and fathers want to invite half the golf club or the entire darts team, while mothers want to see a couple of dozen members of the amateur dramatic society on the list, leaving little room for friends of the couple. Once again, how accommodating you decide to be will depend on your relationship with your parents and how much you want to please them; either suggest a fair allocation, with equal numbers of parents' friends and your friends, or arrange an evening party for friends.

Couples who are making their own wedding arrangements can balance the list in the way that suits them best, but if you are following more traditional lines, where the two mothers make separate lists, then the bride's mother should decide on the total number of guests and suggest that the groom's mother draws up a list for half that number.

You may know that some close friends have family or work commitments that will prevent them from accepting your invitation, or relatives who are too old or infirm to make the journey, but if they come within the range of those you are inviting, they should be sent invitations anyway. Make sure that you include them in your calculations in case they surprise you by accepting.

You will probably need to decide whether or not you will include children on your list. If there are so many children in your family that you can see the reception disintegrating into a shambles as they all run riot, you might decide not to invite the under-fives or the under-tens and you could send a personal note explaining this to the mothers involved. Another possiblity is inviting only children of relatives, but if your second cousin can bring her offspring while those of your oldest friend are excluded, it may cause resentment. Instead, you might try enlisting the help of some teenage guests to keep the children amused or even entertain them in another room.

Counting the cost

Weddings can be very costly and your choice of clothes, the length of your guest list and the place chosen for the reception will probably depend on what you want to spend. Listing the possible costs early on, before you make any firm decisions, is sound policy. Divide them into sections like 'clothes', 'reception' and so on, then you can look at the estimated total for each section and, if you need to prune, decide whether you would rather do without the full regalia of the traditional white wedding and keep the hotel reception; keep the choir and bellringers and invite a dozen less people; settle for a cheaper honeymoon and have everything you ever wanted on the day; or perhaps make economies by hiring instead of buying your dress, making the cake yourself or asking a friend to make it. Make your own list, using the guidelines below, then check on standard charges at the church or register office and talk to local hotels and firms to get an idea of the costs of reception, photographs and so on.

Costs of the ceremony
Minister's fee
Organist's fee
Verger's fee
Choir
Bellringers
Registrar's certificate or licence

Clothes
Bride's dress
Headdress
Shoes
Hire of morning dress
Bridesmaids' dresses
Going-away outfit

Reception
Cake
Hire of venue
Buffet meal
Wedding breakfast
Drinks
Music

Honeymoon
Air fares
Hotels

Transport
Insurance
Spending money

Stationery
Invitations
Service leaflets
Menus
Place cards
Thank-you notes

Flowers
Bride's bouquet
Bridesmaid's bouquets
Corsages
Buttonholes
Church flowers
Reception flowers

Miscellaneous
Photos
Video
Tape recording
Transport to and from church
Rings
Gifts for attendants

When to book

It is possible to arrange wedding ceremony, reception and honey-moon at a couple of weeks' notice but it takes both stamina and luck. It is certainly out of the question if you plan something elaborate. If you want to book your reception at the only hotel in town or order a fleet of white Rolls Royces for the wedding transport, you need to plan well ahead.

Remember that hotels can only hold one, or possibly two, wedding receptions in a day, so summer Saturdays can be booked up months in advance. If you have your eye on one special venue, try to book five or six months ahead. Of course, before you book the hotel you need to book the church, and here, too, the earlier the better, especially if you want one of the most popular times of day.

Photographers and car hire companies both have long lists of bookings for peak wedding times, so it is a good idea to stake your claim as soon as your main arrangements have been made. If you are hiring your wedding dress, try to make your booking two to three months ahead, to give yourself maximum choice. Printed invitations should be ordered at least nine weeks ahead, so that you can send them out in good time, before half your guests have made other plans for that weekend. Eight weeks is usually sufficient time for making arrangements with the florist and for hiring morning suits.

The stag party

Most couples give little thought to a stag party until the last minute with the result that, all too often, both groom and best man arrive for the ceremony pale and shaky, very much the worse for wear from the night before.

Traditionally the stag night was held the evening before the wedding, as a celebration of the groom's last night of freedom before he is locked into the shackles of wife, dishwashing and home decorating. Drink flowed freely and everyone went home at best merry and at worst legless. As a groom with a headache, or worse, can be a wedding day disaster, it is worth planning the stag night into your schedule early on, fixing it for several days before the big day.

The rule that only unmarried men were invited to the stag night is often ignored nowadays, but it is still usually an event for friends and relatives of around the bridegroom's own age. It is, of course, strictly for men only; if the bride wants to celebrate the last of her 'freedom', she has to organize a similar party for her girlfriends.

The evening can include anything from a full-scale party with entertainment laid on, to a few drinks in the pub with the bridegroom buying only the first round. Of course, it does not have to be organized round alcohol; a restaurant meal with a few light-hearted toasts might be just as enjoyable.

The emphasis is always on informality, so written invitations are not necessary. If speeches are included, two are sufficient and these should take place at the coffee stage of a meal or, at a drinks party, about half way through the evening. The best man will aim for plenty of laughs at the bridegroom's expense and the groom will reply. (See p.111 for advice on speechmaking.)

Who foots the bill

In the past, rules on paying for the wedding were clear. The main burden of cost fell on the bride's family, as a legacy from the days when every bride came to her new husband with a dowry.

Today, when the bride and groom may have been living independently of their families for some time, and their joint income can add up to more than the bride's father is earning, things are very different. Many couples pay for their own weddings, or at least contribute, or the bridegroom's family may want to pay their share.

It is wise to make no initial assumptions about payment, or you may end up with hurt feelings all round. There are still fathers who insist on paying every penny and would be wounded by any other arrangement, but it would be a foolish daughter who *assumes* that is the case. A full and frank discussion of finances right at the beginning will put everyone in the picture and show up any touchy areas where tact will be needed.

Plenty of couples pay for their own weddings, perhaps with the groom paying for the reception and the bride handling the rest of the bills traditionally the province of her family, or simply sharing the expenses as they will once married. One of the biggest advantages of this modern style of marriage is that there is less pressure to bow to the parents' wishes about the style or size of the wedding, just because they are footing the bill.

If the family is paying the lion's share and the couple want to contribute, the bride might buy her own dress and flowers and the groom might pay for the wine at the reception. Some couples keep the reception small, just inviting relatives, and lay on their own party for friends.

An offer from the groom's parents to pay a share of the costs may be accepted with delighted gratitude. On the other hand it may cause a good deal of resentment. Everything depends on the relationship between the families, but they should always feel their way with care.

The best way may be to list all the costs, then hold a family conference to decide who pays what. As a guideline, the traditional division of expenses is as follows:

The bride's family pay for

Engagement and wedding announcements in the press

Wedding stationery: printed invitations, order of service leaflets, menus, place cards, printed thank-you notes if required

Engagement and pre-wedding party, if any

The bride's dress, accessories and going-away clothes

The bridesmaids' and attendants' clothes – these days they would normally make a contribution, at most

Photographs, videos, tape recordings, etc.

Flowers for the church or reception, though churches often have their own floral arrangements and hotels may include flowers in their overall charges

Cars for the bride's family to the church and the bride's parents to the reception

All costs for the reception: catering, hire of hall, cake, wine, entertainment

The bridegroom pays for

Engagement and wedding ring(s)

Marriage licence

Registry office fees or church expenses, including the minister's fee, organist, choir, bellringers and verger

Bride's and bridesmaids' bouquets

Buttonholes for himself, the best man and ushers

Corsages for the two mothers

Presents for the bridesmaids and best man

Cars for himself and the best man to the church – unless the best man is using his own car.

Car for himself and the bride to the reception – though these days the bridal car is normally used

The honeymoon

The bride pays for

The bridegroom's ring, if required

The best man pays for

His own wedding clothes

3

Legal Matters

Getting married means conforming to certain legal regulations and, though these may seem boring compared to the excitement of choosing dresses and arranging honeymoons, it is essential to make sure nothing is overlooked. Failure to check details has meant an ugly last-minute hitch for some happy couples!

The law says that you must be over sixteen before you can marry and if you are under eighteen, you will need your parents' consent. It is the couple's responsibility to see that they have the necessary certificates or licences ready to hand to the registering official on the day.

Weddings can take place between 8.00 a.m. and 6.00 p.m.; the exceptions are Jewish and Quaker weddings and marriages by special licence and Registrar General's licence. Two witnesses must be present but they do not have to be friends or relatives: complete strangers brought in from the street will do just as well.

Church of England weddings

Marriage by banns
This is the most popular – and the cheapest – way of marrying in the Church of England. This means that the banns must be read out on three consecutive Sundays before the wedding can take place. Once this has been done the couple are free to marry any time within the next three months. If for some reason the wedding does not take place within that time, the banns have to be read again.

If either the bride or groom lives in a different parish, then the banns must be read in both churches and the clergyman whose church is not being used must provide a certificate saying that the banns have been duly called. Without that certificate, the officiating clergyman cannot perform the ceremony.

The whole idea of calling banns is that everyone should know who is planning to marry, so if the name by which everyone calls you is different from the name on your birth certificate, the banns should be called in your usual name, or include both.

Marriage by common licence
People often talk about marrying by 'special licence', but special licences are rare, and they are much more likely to be referring to common licence. This is more expensive but quicker than waiting for banns to be called. Provided that either the man or woman has lived in the parish for at least fifteen days before making the application, the banns are waived and the couple can marry immediately.

The local clergyman may be able to issue the licence himself but if not, he will be able to direct you to the surrogate granting licences in the diocese. When applying, either the man or the woman must appear in person to sign a declaration stating that there is no legal reason why the marriage should not take place and that the residence qualification has been complied with. Residence does not mean that you have to sleep within the parish every one of those fifteen nights – it is sufficient if your name appears on the electoral roll.

Marriage by special licence
Special licences are issued only in exceptional circumstances – for instance, if either the bride or groom is too ill to attend church. It is issued only by the Archbishop of Canterbury at the Faculty Office, 1 The Sanctuary, Westminster, London SW1, and means that the wedding can take place in a building (such as a hospital) not normally licensed for marriages.

Register office weddings

Marriage by superintendent registrar's certificate
Notice must be given to the district superintendent registrar, who will complete a form giving the names of the couple, their addresses and ages, and ending with a declaration, to be signed by one of the

parties to the marriage, stating that there is no legal reason why the marriage cannot take place. If both the bride and groom live in the same district, then only one of them need give notice and sign the declaration; if they live in different districts, each must make a separate declaration before their local registrar. Before giving notice, you must have lived in the area for at least seven days.

If either of you is under eighteen, you will need to produce written consent from your parents or guardians before you can give notice. If your parents are abroad, make sure they have their signatures properly witnessed, preferably by a consular official.

The registrar will make an entry in his notice book and will issue the certificate twenty-one days later. The marriage may then take place *within three months of the date of notice*, so if the wedding is postponed, keep a careful eye on the dates.

Marriage by superintendent registrar's certificate and licence

This costs more than twice as much as marriage by certificate only and is for people in a hurry. Both bride and groom must be in England or Wales, or have their usual residence in England or Wales on the day notice is given. Only one of you need give notice, whether you live in the same district or not, but one of you must have lived in that district for fifteen days immediately before giving notice and the wedding must take place in that district.

There must be one clear day (excluding Sunday, Christmas Day or Good Friday) between the day the registrar makes his entry in his notice book and the day he issues the certificate. The marriage can then take place at any time within three months *from the day on which the notice was entered*.

Marriage by Registrar General's licence

This is rare, but can be granted if either bride or groom is seriously ill and not expected to recover. Then the Registrar General may grant a licence for the marriage to be held in the house or hospital where the patient is lying.

Other denominations

Marriages are by certificate or certificate and licence, provided the minister is 'an authorized person' and the building is registered by the Superintendent Registrar of Marriages for the purpose of conducting marriage services.

Not all clergymen in Free Churches are 'authorized persons' and in this case, the registrar must be present in order to register the marriage. Members of non-Christian religions – Sikhs and Hindus for instance – often prefer, for the sake of convenience, to arrange a civil marriage a day, or a few hours, before the religious ceremony.

Jewish weddings

Jewish couples need to give notice to the registrar, or two registrars if they live in different districts, but the marriage may take place in a synagogue, a private house or even out of doors.

In addition to complying with the law of the land, the couple must obtain permission of the Chief Rabbi and local synagogue officials will advise on the procedure. Both parties must be Jews and will be required to produce evidence that their parents were married according to Jewish rites. If either bride or groom is not of Jewish birth, evidence of proselytization is necessary.

Weddings may not take place on the Sabbath – from sunset on Friday to sunset on Saturday – or on certain festival days, but otherwise it can take place at any time of day.

Quaker weddings

Couples marrying in accordance with the rites of the Society of Friends will require a registrar's certificate. They must also give notice to the registering officer at their Friend's Meeting House. The marriage may take place wherever the regular Quaker meeting is held in the area.

Naval marriages

The Naval Marriage Act of 1908 made special arrangements for those serving in the Royal Navy, because of the difficulty of giving sufficient notice of marriage when you are on the high seas. In this case the banns can be published by the ship's chaplain or commanding officer if the wedding is to be in church. If it is to take place in a register office or nonconformist chapel, notice may be given to the commanding officer in place of the registrar and he will issue a certificate after twenty-one days.

Notice must be given in the usual way by the other person, or the banns must be read.

Sadly, the idea that a ship's captain can perform a marriage ceremony for members of the crew or passengers is a Hollywood myth. The captain is not authorized to perform the duties reserved for state-appointed registrars.

When the bride or groom lives in Scotland

If one of you lives in England or Wales, where you plan to marry, and the other in Scotland, then the partner in the south proceeds as normal. The person coming from Scotland will need a Scottish registrar's certificate showing that there is no impediment to the marriage, whether it takes place in church or register office. (See section on Scottish marriages, p.32.)

When the bride or groom lives in Ireland

If one of you lives in Northern Ireland but you plan to marry in England or Wales, the situation is as described above and the person coming from Northern Ireland will need a certificate issued by a District Registrar of Marriages. (See p.33.)

If one of the partners lives in the Irish Republic and is coming to Britain for the wedding, that person must come here and establish the necessary residence qualification before notice may be given to the registrar.

Marriage of foreign nationals

If either of the marriage partners has their home in another country, it is important to remember that a British marriage will not necessarily be valid in the home country unless the legal requirements of that country have been met, in addition to those of English law. This should be checked with the consular representative of the country concerned.

Sometimes, unscrupulous agents claim that they can arrange marriages quickly, without the usual residence qualifications being met, but the registering authorities warn that any false statements on the marriage notice can leave the couple open to charges of perjury.

Second marriages

There is no legal limit on the number of times anyone may marry and, so long as a divorced person produces the *decree nisi*, there are no problems over arranging a register office wedding and the procedures are exactly the same as for single people.

The difficulties arise when the bride and groom, one or both of them divorced, want to marry in church. The Roman Catholic church does not allow 're-marriage' for a divorced person whose partner is still living. However, if the previous marriage can be declared invalid – in other words, in ecclesiastical eyes it never existed – then the divorcee is regarded as unmarried and will be able to marry in church. If your first marriage was in a register office, you may be able to have it declared null and void but this does not apply if the first marriage was in a Protestant church.

Many Church of England ministers take the same position as Roman Catholics and would not consider hearing a bride or groom making vows 'until death us do part' for the second time around. Some used to take the view that only the 'innocent party' could re-marry in church but since the law allowed divorce by consent, that idea has become largely redundant. There are clergymen who will take a view based on the individual circumstances of the couple but you are dependent on finding a sympathetic ear in a local parish.

The Free churches are traditionally more liberal and normally allow a divorced person with an ex-spouse still living to re-marry in church. Of course, if you have never set foot in your local Methodist or Baptist church, your chances depend on convincing the minister concerned that you have good and sincere reasons for wanting a church ceremony for a second marriage and aren't interested only in the pleasant setting and the organ music.

If you are unable to arrange a church wedding but feel there is something lacking without a religious ceremony, a service of blessing can be a good compromise solution. This is a simple service, usually including hymns, prayers, a bible reading and a blessing, but not an exchange of marriage vows. It can take place any time after the civil ceremony, but often the bridal couple, with their parents and a couple of close friends acting as best man and bridesmaid, go to the church for the blessing before joining their guests at the reception.

Scottish marriages

Couples who wanted to marry quickly and without all the restrictions of English law used to elope to Gretna Green, just few miles over the border. All they had to do was to make a declaration before two witnesses and they were man and wife.

Many couples still go to Gretna Green for a mock ceremony over the anvil at the Old Smithy but these days it is only a romantic gesture. Since the Marriage (Scotland) Act of 1977, the rules are much stricter, but they still differ from the regulations in England and Wales.

In Scotland you can marry if you are sixteen or over; under-eighteens do not need the consent of their parents. You need two witnesses aged sixteen or over, but you do not need to have lived in Scotland before the marriage.

You can be married by a registrar, in which case the marriage will normally take place in his office, though if there are special circumstances – serious illness for instance – he can perform the ceremony elsewhere.

Banns are not necessary for church weddings, and unlike in England and Wales, ministers can perform the ceremony at a private house, a hotel or anywhere else.

Both bride and groom must obtain a marriage notice form from any registrar of births, deaths and marriages in Scotland. When the notices are completed they should be taken to the registrar in the district where the marriage is to take place. You will also need to produce your birth certificates and, if either of you has been married before, the death certificate of the former spouse, or your divorce decree. If either of you live outside the United Kingdom, you will need evidence to show that there is no legal reason in your own country why you should not be married. If any your documents are in a foreign language, you will need to produce a certified translation.

Notice must be given at least fourteen clear days before the marriage and lists of proposed marriages are displayed outside registrars' offices.

If one of you lives in England or Wales, but you are marrying someone who lives in Scotland, you do not have to go there to give notice. Instead you apply to the Superintendent Registrar in your district for a certificate which will be accepted in place of notice in Scotland. Your partner gives notice in the usual way.

When you have both given notice, the registrar will prepare a marriage schedule, which he will keep if you are marrying in his office. If you are marrying in church one of you must collect it in person, and it must be produced to the minister before he can perform the marriage. Immediately after the ceremony the schedule is signed by bride and groom, two witnesses and the person who conducted the wedding. It must then be returned to the registrar within three days so that he can register the marriage.

Marriage in Northern Ireland

In Northern Ireland, notice of marriage must be given to the District Registrar of Marriages. It can take place by banns, licence, special licence, registrar's certificate or District Registrar's licence.

Notices issued in Northern Ireland are valid in England and Wales and vice versa but marriage by licence in a register office in England and Wales is not possible if either of the couple is resident in Northern Ireland.

Marriage abroad

If you marry abroad your marriage will be valid under British law, so long as it is legally valid in the country where it took place and does not infringe any of the British regulations – for instance age, freedom to marry and the relationship of the bride and groom.

There is nothing to stop you joining the 50,000 Americans who marry in Las Vegas each year. Weddings there are simplicity itself:

you apply to the County Clerk for a licence, then go along to one of the two dozen wedding chapels – perhaps the Hitching Post or the Chapel of the Stars – and find yourself married ten minutes later. Some travel companies offer complete wedding packages, including jet flights to some romantic location, wedding ceremony, photographs, champagne reception – and all the necessary documentation.

When planning to marry abroad, you need to check the legal requirements in the country involved very carefully and leave nothing to chance. You will probably need your birth certificate and a certified document stating that there is no legal impediment to your marriage. Check with the consulate for any regulations relating to age, health or residence, proof of no criminal convictions and so on.

Prohibited marriages

The law forbids marriages between people who are closely related. You may not marry your:
mother, adoptive mother, former adoptive mother, father, adoptive or former adoptive father, daughter, adoptive or former adoptive daughter, son, adoptive or former adoptive son, father's mother, father's father, mother's mother, mother's father, son's daughter, son's son, daughter's daughter, daughter's son, sister, brother, wife's mother, husband's father, wife's daughter, husband's son, father's wife, mother's husband, son's wife, daughter's husband, father's father's wife, father's mother's husband, mother's father's wife, mother's mother's husband, wife's father's mother, husband's father's father, wife's mother's mother, husband's father's father, wife's son's daughter, husband's son's son, wife's daughter's daughter, husband's daughter's son, son's son's wife, son's daughter's husband, daughter's son's wife, daughter's daughter's husband, father's sister, father's brother, mother's sister, mother's brother, brother's daughter, brother's son, sister's daughter, sister's son.

In this century there have been several changes in the law prohibiting marriage between relatives. In 1907 it became legal for a man to marry his brother's widow or for a widower to marry his dead wife's sister. In 1921 it became legal for a widow to marry her dead husband's brother or the widower of her dead sister. In 1960, the law changed to allow a divorced man or woman to marry the sister or brother of their ex-spouse.

There are still some ministers who are unwilling to marry such couples and they are not obliged to do so. The answer is to seek out a more up-to-date clergyman or marry in a register office, where there will be no such problem.

Invalid marriages

Marriages are invalid – in other words, they are legally regarded as never having existed – if the partners are relatives not allowed to marry (see the above list), if either the bride or groom is under sixteen years of age, if one of them has married before and not obtained a divorce, or if they were not of sufficiently sound mind at the time of the marriage to understand what they were doing.

Changing your name

You do not have to take your husband's name when you marry, though the majority of brides still do so, either because it is all tied up with the experience of getting married or because it simply makes life easier.

However, more and more women do prefer to keep their maiden name. Some feel that they are giving up an important part of their own identity by changing their name, others are well known by one name in their profession and feel that changing may put them at a disadvantage.

If you keep your own name, you need to be prepared for plenty of irritation from government departments who have difficulty coming to terms with the idea and insist on calling you Mrs Sproggett when you keep telling them your name is Ms Crusty. It can also cause some embarrassment if you travel in more strait-laced countries with passports in different names.

Using both names can be a compromise solution, as then the Inland Revenue and your mother-in-law can write to you as Mrs Sproggett but in day-to-day working life you answer to Ms Crusty. It can cause difficulties if you are called upon to identify yourself in one name and the only documents you have on you are in another, or you are writing cheques in one name for people who know you by another. However, this is becoming much more common and, so long as you aren't looking shifty, few people will comment.

An alternative is to follow the American custom of adopting both names, but this works better if you turn into a Winter Evans or a Thurston Brown than if you find yourself a Crusty Sproggett.

If you do decide to change your name, make sure you notify your tax inspector, your bank manager, credit card companies, and the Driver and Vehicle Licensing Centre for changes on your driving licence and vehicle registration documents, building society and insurance companies.

If you are going abroad on honeymoon and want your passport changed to your married name, make sure you apply to the Passport Office, Clive House, Petty France, London SW1, in plenty of time.

4

Setting the Scene

There are many different styles of wedding. Most take a great deal of careful planning, and laying on a formal wedding with all the trimmings can be like staging a major stage production. But whether you follow tradition or do your own thing, you will want to set the scene perfectly to suit your chosen style. The choice of the right clothes, flowers, music and even transport will mean that your wedding day is a triumphant success.

The wedding outfits

The bride

The traditional 'white' wedding is still the most popular among church brides but it is by no means obligatory. Day clothes are just as acceptable or, if you opt for a long dress, train and veil, they can be in other colours: cream or oyster, or deeper shades if you prefer. The most important thing is to choose clothes that will feel right on the day and match the style of your wedding.

The idea that white is for virgins only was jettisoned long ago and many a pregnant bride has been glad of the loose, flowing lines of a carefully chosen wedding dress. Older brides, or those marrying for a second time, are entitled to wear white if they wish, though cream is a more usual choice and there are many alternative colours – perhaps gold, rich blue or russet colours for an autumn ceremony.

Various denominations have their own preferred dress custom, with the traditional white dress with all the trimmings usual in the Roman Catholic and High Churches, as well as at Jewish weddings, while the Free Churches are more likely to put the emphasis on simplicity.

The bride's accessories need to complement the style of the dress, whether formal or informal. Traditionally, a veil goes with a white dress and can be shoulder-length, fingertip length, floor-length or 'cathedral' length, when it extends beyond the length of the train. If a bride chooses to wear a veil, it should be down as she enters the church, then lifted either before the ceremony or in the vestry so that she walks down the aisle with her face uncovered. Headdresses can be worn with or without a veil and a garland of flowers is a popular choice, though a single bloom makes an attractive alternative.

A register office bride can still wear the full regalia if she wishes, though a train is normally omitted as there will not be room to accommodate it properly, and no chance to display it to the full. Veils are seldom worn, as there is no suitable time at which to pull them back. Many people choose a different style which can be simple or elaborate, long or short, with or without a hat, with or without flowers. Many women choose wide-brimmed, 'Ascot' style hats but it should be borne in mind that these can cast shadows over the face, which may not improve the look of the photographs.

The bridegroom and best man

All the men of the wedding party should dress with the same degree of formality. Strictly speaking, when the bride wears white the groom should wear morning dress, and this means that the best man, the two fathers and the ushers must follow suit. Morning suits consist of black morning coat, grey pin-striped trousers, grey waistcoat, grey tie, white shirt, black socks and shoes. For weddings, a grey coat with tails is often substituted and sometimes a cravat is worn instead of a tie. Strictly speaking, the outfit is completed by a grey topper, which can be worn on the walk up the church path and for the photographs. However, as the topper can be a nuisance for the rest of the time – too tall to wear n the car and needing to be stored along with other identical toppers to cause confusion at the end of the celebrations – some bridegrooms decide to dispense with it altogether. As few men have morning dress hanging in their wardrobe, the whole outfit, complete with topper, gloves and tie, is usually hired. Most firms offer a hire period extending from Friday to Monday.

Jewish bridegrooms wear a dinner jacket and black tie, but in other denominations, a two- or three-piece lounge suit is sufficiently smart for the occasion. Morning dress is not unknown for register office ceremonies but lounge suits are more usual, even when the bride wears traditional white.

The bridesmaids

When planning dresses for bridesmaids, keep in mind that on the day you will be seen as a group. The style of their clothes should follow the style of the wedding dress: frills and flounces on the bridesmaids would look quite wrong alongside a bride dressed with classic simplicity. If the bride's dress is in Victorian or Edwardian style, then the bridesmaids' dresses should echo this.

When bridesmaids are paying for their own dresses, they will want a say in what is chosen, and in any case, you should plan clothes that will take account of their individual looks, height and colouring. It would, for example, be unwise – as well as unkind – to force a fat little cousin into a tight-fitting dress with puffed sleeves.

Pastel colours like pink, pale blue, lilac and peach are always popular but darker colours like turquoise or deep red can look good on girls with the right colouring. Patterns – flowers, stripes, spots or checks – can also be very effective. When the attendants are of different ages, try two tones of the same colour, or a plain dress for the older girl and a flowered version for the younger. If you are planning a whole row of bridesmaids, a deepening shade from the little ones in, say, pale pink to the oldest (or tallest) in deep rose can be very effective.

Dresses for adult bridesmaids are normally the same length as that of the bride but children's dresses can be long or short. It is usually wiser not to expect very small children to manage floor-length dresses.

Attention to detail pays off when planning clothes for the attendants. Check on accessories, hairstyles, shoes, stockings, socks and make-up to make sure that everything blends together to enhance the overall effect of the bridal party.

The mothers

Some mothers like to keep their wedding outfit a closely guarded secret until the day but there are pitfalls in this approach. Both the bride's and bridegroom's mother will be central figures in the photographs, standing close together on the receiving line and sitting on the top table at the reception, so if they choose clashing colours, or one is far more formally dressed than the other, the outcome can be disappointment and embarrassment. It will be just as bad if they turn up in an identical colour, looking like two bookends in the formal group photos. They should also ensure that their outfits tone with the colours worn by the bridesmaids. Try to persuade them to liaise at least as far as colour and style is concerned. Strictly speaking, the bride's mother has first choice.

Double weddings
The whole bridal party should dress with the same degree of formality. The two brides can choose different styles but dresses, trains and veils should be the same length. The bridesmaids' dresses, too, need to be the same length, though the colours can be different, providing they harmonize.

The flowers

Flowers have been part of our wedding customs throughout the centuries: in medieval tradition girls carried garlands of wheat before the bride to ensure the fertility. No wedding seems complete without them and ideally the colours or theme of the bridal flowers should be echoed throughout the day, in the church and reception room.

When you talk to the florist, give as much information as possible about the colour and style of dresses, take along sample pieces of fabric and any magazine pictures of bouquets or arrangements that might have caught your eye. Usually the flowers are chosen to tone with the colours of bride's and bridesmaids' dresses, but you might consider taking your theme from the colours of flowers available in your chosen wedding month: for instance, a gentle primrose in April, the soft pink of early roses in May, or the delicate sweet pea shades of June.

Flowers for the bridal party
Traditionally, the bride carries a bouquet, though a prayerbook with a spray of flowers attached is a popular alternative. At a formal wedding, the bouquet needs to be large enough to balance a long, sweeping dress and veil, though visually, it would be a mistake to dwarf a small bride with a huge bouquet. A simple, short dress will

probably look better with a neat posy. Keep in mind the type of flowers that best complement your own looks and personality, whether sophisticated or dainty, exotic or simple. The bride may also choose a headdress of flowers or wear flowers twined in her hair, but remember that fresh flowers can only be attached at the last moment, otherwise they may wilt before the end of the day.

When choosing bouquets and headdresses for bridesmaids, bear in mind the colouring of the girls themselves, as well as the colour of their dresses. Flowers for young bridesmaids should be light and easy to carry. Flowerballs, rather than posies, may be a good idea; children often find them more interesting and they are less likely to be dropped or crushed. An alternative for a child bridesmaid is a basket of flowers, which makes a pretty memento of the day.

Buttonholes are worn by the bridegroom, both fathers, the best man and the ushers. Traditionally these are white carnations but roses (perhaps in the same colour as the bride's bouquet) or lilies of the valley are attractive possibilities.

Flowers for the rest of the day
You may or may not have the opportunity of choosing flowers to decorate the church but, if you do, take the style of the church into account. The larger the church, the larger and more striking the arrangements will need to be; in a smaller church it might be better to concentrate the floral arrangement in one place, perhaps along-side the altar, as this will be the focus of all eyes. White flowers can lighten a dark church but if the bride wears a stark white fabric, the softer, creamier tones of white flowers may not set it off to best advantage. In many of the Free Churches warmer pink or peach shades are better suited to the light walls and woodwork.

Features like the pulpit or font might be singled out for decoration, if the minister agrees, and floral decorations on the pew ends give an air of lavish abundance to the ceremony and carry the scent of flowers all the way down the aisle. At a Jewish wedding, garlands of flowers decorating the canopy can be very effective.

At a hotel reception, the flower arrangements will probably be part of the package deal, so be sure to discuss suitable colours and styles with the banqueting manager when you make the other arrangements. (See Chapter 7.)

Flowers in season

When you specify particular flowers for bouquets or floral arrangements, bear in mind that there is always a possibility that the florist will not be able to obtain them at the crucial moment, so you may need to have an alternative choice. Some of the suitable flowers obtainable by season are listed below, but remember that the seasons sometimes overlap:

Available all year round:
Carnation
Chrysanthemum
Freesia
Gladioli
Iris
Lily
Rose
Orchid
Stephanotis

Summer
Aster
Campanula
Cornflower
Daisy
Delphinium
Fuschia
Lupin
Marigold
Paeony
Pink
Sweet-william
Stocks
Sweet peas

Spring
Anemone
Camellia
Daffodil
Hyacinth
Jasmine
Lilac
Lily of the valley
Narcissus
Philadelphus
Polyanthus
Primrose

Autumn
Alstroemeria
Dahlia
Hydrangea
Morning glory

Winter
Snowdrop
Winter jasmine

Flower lore

In folklore, flowers have always been thought to have their own language, each conveying its own message. For centuries orange blossom has been a symbol of fertility as well as good luck and happiness, making it the perfect wedding flower, closely followed by the rose. In ancient times roses were dedicated to Venus, so they have always been the symbol of happy love.

If you care about the meaning of flowers, you might want to include in the bridal bouquet and other arrangements: lilies (purity and dignity), sweet-william (happiness), snowdrops (hope), tulips (a declaration of love), lilies of the valley (true happiness), violets (modesty), daisies (innocence), dahlias (dignity and elegance), jasmine (good nature), Canterbury bells (constancy), forget-me-nots (remembrance and fidelity), honeysuckle (generous love), pinks (pure love), lilac (young love).

Among the flowers that believers in flower lore might prefer to avoid are marigolds (grief), narcissus (self-centredness), hydrangeas (boastfulness), iris (indifference), and daffodil (self-love). Some yellow flowers also have unfortunate meanings: yellow roses signify unfaithfulness and yellow tulips hopeless love.

The photographs

Most couples look on the wedding photographs as a souvenir to treasure, so it is worth taking trouble to ensure that the job is done well. Relying on snapshots taken by friends and relatives is seldom satisfactory: cameras fail, films get fogged in the changing or lost in the post and the occasional amateur photographer has been known to drink too much champagne and picture feet instead of faces.

Ask around among friends or acquaintances who have married recently and ask to look at their wedding pictures. If you do not have a word-of-mouth recommendation, shop around the local photographers and see examples of their work. The most expensive is not always the best; styles vary and you should be able to select the one that most appeals to you.

Methods of charging vary a good deal. Some firms charge for each print but not for the job itself, some set an overall charge for the day, including a set number of prints, in which case you need to know whether they select the prints or provide you with a contact sheet so that you can choose those you like the best. You may pay a smaller fee if you allow the photographer to circulate the contact sheets at the reception and take orders from the guests – and it can be interesting for guests to see the range of photos, especially if they are never likely to see your album.

If you are planning a small wedding, paying for each print may be the better deal; if it is a large affair and you want scores of photos taken, you will probably be better off with a package.

You will need to tell the photographer whether you want colour or black and white and whether you want 'candid' pictures as well as the formal shots. Sometimes colour for the formal poses and black and white for the informal shots of the wind carrying away Auntie Jean's hat, the pageboys fighting, or grandpa snoozing over his champagne, works well.

Think about whether you want photos taken at the bride's home before she sets out (if so, allow an extra half hour in the preparation time), whether you want photos of the guests taken as they arrive and whether you can have pictures taken inside the church. You will need to check this with the minister: some have no objection so long as photos are not taken during the ceremony itself; some allow non-flash photography only; others object to the whole idea.

If you are planning some formal groups outside the church or register office, make sure you have an alternative plan in case of bad weather. You will not look your best shivering with cold or sheltering under umbrellas and the guests can lose enthusiasm if they are kept standing about for half an hour in drizzle or a cutting north wind. Register offices are not always in the prettiest spots, so you might want to consider a nearby park, an attractive square or friends' garden as an alternative. If you are unlucky enough to be faced with the choice of a narrow pavement in the high street or the pocket handkerchief of grass outside the town hall, it might be worth allowing half an hour at the photographer's studio before beginning the celebrations.

Make your booking well ahead, especially if you are marrying on a summer Saturday, when the good photographers have plenty of work. Confirm all the details in writing and double check a few weeks later to make sure there are no hitches.

Professionals will know all the standard groups and poses but it is up to you to tell them if you want anything you feel might be outside the usual range. If you have a friend or relative you can depend on to produce a good set of pictures and decide to rely on him or her, make out a list, along the lines of the one below, to make sure nothing is missed out:

Before the ceremony
The bride putting the finishing touches to her preparations
The bridesmaids, or the bride's mother, helping the bride to get ready
The bride and her father leaving the house

The groom and the best man arriving at the church
Each guest arriving
The bride's father helping her out of the car
The bridesmaids at the church door
The bride and her father approaching the church
The bride and her father going down the aisle
The bride and groom standing at the altar
The ceremony itself
The procession leaving the church or the bride and groom leaving the register office
The bride and groom outside the church or register office
The bride and groom, best man and bridesmaids
The bride and groom, attendants and both sets of parents
The bride and groom with all the family members
The bridal party with all the guests, if numbers permit
The cake
The receiving line at the reception
The top table once the guests are seated
The toasts
Cutting the cake
The bride throwing her bouquet
The couple leaving the reception

Videos

Video recordings of weddings are becoming increasingly popular and make a delightful keepsake, particularly if the minister will allow you to include the ceremony, but they are best left to the experts; there are no chances of a re-run if the result is a disappointment. Choose a firm that specializes in weddings and make sure you see examples of the finished product. Notice whether the lighting and sound was satisfactory all the way through and whether the video crew have managed to make the wedding party and guests look natural or if they are stiffly posed throughout.

If possible, visit the church and the site of the reception with the video crew, at the same time of the day the wedding is to take place. Check on camera angles and any additional lighting that might be necessary, ask whether they will use portable cameras without trailing wires and transmitting microphones which will capture the sound adequately when, for instance, you are exchanging your vows.

When comparing prices between firms, check on any extras included in the package: some offer a professional bridal makeup. Sometimes the firm providing the photographer can offer a video service too, perhaps with an advantageous price if you take both services.

Transport

There are various luxurious ways of travelling to your wedding – perhaps a white Rolls-Royce, a vintage car or a horse-drawn carriage. However, many families manage perfectly well with their own or borrowed cars, with or without white ribbons for the occasion.

The large cars hired from specialist wedding firms have the advantage of plenty of room to accommodate long flowing dresses. Two will normally be required: one to take the bride and her father to the church, the other for the bridesmaids and possibly the bride's mother, unless she travels separately, escorted by a male relative. The first car will then take the bride and groom on to the reception, the second transports the attendants. The best man will usually drive the bridegroom to the ceremony in his own, or the groom's, car. Be sure not to forget that the bride's parents need transport to the reception, and should not be reduced to begging lifts outside the church.

It is not obligatory to arrange transport for guests but if people are coming long distances and arriving at railway stations some miles distant, it is polite to make arrangements to have some transport to meet them. You can either enlist the help of friends with cars or ask your guests if they would like taxis booked.

When the reception is to be held nearby, it can be very effective if the bridal party lead their guests on foot (take advice from the police if this means crossing busy roads), but be prepared with an alternative plan in case of bad weather. If the reception is not within walking distance, make sure that guests with cars are ready to offer lifts.

Register office weddings can follow a similar pattern if they are full dress events, but if the style of the day is simple, the wedding party may simply arrange to meet at the registrar's office. Alternatively, the bride might travel with one of the witnesses and the groom with the other.

Choosing the music

The atmosphere of a church wedding will depend to a large extent on the music you choose, so it is worth taking the time to plan a balanced, effective programme, rather than simply leaving it to the organist to play what he plays every Saturday.

Of course, your choice will be governed by the quality of the organ and the skill of the organist: if both are indifferent, then it is better to stick to simpler, more familiar pieces of music rather than branch out into something too ambitious. Most organists will try to please you, even if it means practising an unfamiliar piece, but remember that both organist and choir will probably perform best in pieces they know and enjoy.

If the church has no resident choir, a local school or choral society may be able to provide one. If you are not having a choir and you can't rely on your family to hit all the notes with perfect accuracy, it might be wise not to have too much singing in the service, and if you are marrying in a small country church, there is no point in picking something that would need Westminster Abbey to do it justice.

The music is most effective if it builds up all the way through, so that the climax comes when the bride and groom walk down the aisle together. In the Church of England ceremony, there are five musical phases to think about: before the bride's entrance; the procession to the altar; the hymns during the service; while the register is signed; and finally, the recessional.

Before the entry of the bride, guests will be arriving, finding their seats and their order of service, so you need music strong enough to cover a certain amount of scuffling and create a sense of occasion. Works by Bach, Handel and Purcell all serve to put the congregation in the right mood.

The old favourite, the 'Bridal March' from Wagner's *Lohengrin*, associated with the words 'Here comes the bride', has become so hackneyed that it is rather out of favour these days. Stirring alternatives are Jeremiah Clarke's *Trumpet Voluntary* or Handel's

Arrival of the Queen of Sheba, or you could choose a good, strong hymn like *Love Divine, All Loves Excelling* or *O Worship the King*, so that the members of the congregation feel they are involved in the ceremony from the first moment.

Practise walking to the music you have in mind before making the final selection, and make sure you will be happy with the tempo. You should also keep in mind the length of the aisle and how long it will take to walk it, so that you are not in the position of walking the last few steps in silence after the music finishes, or having to wait for it to end.

Most people pick their favourite hymns – at one fashionable wedding the guests found themselves singing *Fight the Good Fight* – but make sure your hymns do not all sound alike. If you pick *Love Divine, All Loves Excelling*, then avoid *Praise My Soul, the King of Heaven*; they both have four-line verses and similar rhythm.

Two hymns and a psalm are usually sufficient and unless you have a choir to carry the singing, it is wise to choose hymns that most people will know and have the psalm spoken rather than sung. Popular psalms for weddings are Psalm 67, 'Lord be merciful to us and bless us'; Psalm 121, 'I will lift up mine eyes'; Psalm 128, 'Blessed are they that fear the Lord and walk in his ways'; and Psalm 23, 'The Lord is my shepherd'. If Psalm 23 is to be sung, remember to specify which setting you want, either Crimond or Brother James's Air.

While the couple sign the register in the vestry, there is nothing for the congregation to do but admire the flowers and criticize one another's outfits, so sweet, fairly restful music is suitable. Bach's *Jesu Joy of Man's Desiring* or *Sheep May Safely Graze* are both pleasantly soothing, either as an organ solo or sung by the choir. A good choir can do justice to Brahm's *How Lovely is Thy Dwelling Place*.

For the procession down the aisle, one of the best-used pieces is Mendelssohn's wedding march from *A Midsummer Night's Dream*, with its impressive fanfare. The Prince and Princess of Wales came down the aisle to Elgar's *Pomp and Circumstance March No.4*. Widor's *Toccata*, used by both Princess Alexandra and the Duchess of Kent at their weddings, sounds splendid, but only if the church has a large modern organ to do it justice. If your church is not that well equipped, Purcell's *Trumpet Tune* can give much the same effect. Couples often choose Verdi's 'Grand March' from *Aida*, but that is meant to celebrate a military victory!

Of course, you may want to dispense with the organist and ignore the traditional music altogether, but this is a matter you need to sort out with a sympathetic minister. Some clergymen will let you import guitars and sing folk music instead of hymns, or perhaps include a popular ballad in the service; many others will not.

The following list, though not comprehensive, will give you some ideas for suitable wedding music:

Before the service

Bach	*Jesu Joy of Man's Desiring*
	Any of the *Choral Preludes*
Elgar	'Nimrod' from the *Enigma Variations*
Handel	*Water Music*
	'Aria' from *10th Organ Concerto*
Purcell	*Prelude in G*

The entrance of the bride

Bliss	*A Wedding Fanfare*
Beethoven	'Hallelujah Chorus' from the *Mount of Olives*
Clarke	*Trumpet Voluntary*
Handel	*Arrival of the Queen of Sheba*
Hollins	*A Trumpet Minuet*
Mozart	'Wedding March' from *The Marriage of Figaro*
Parry	*Bridal March*
Purcell	*Fanfare*
Stanley	'Trumpet Voluntary' from *Suite in D*
Wagner	'Bridal March' from *Lohengrin*

Hymns

Come Down, O Love Divine
Dear Lord and Father of Mankind
God Be in My Head
Lead Us, Heavenly Father, Lead Us
Love Divine, All Loves Excelling
O Perfect Love
O Father All-creating
Praise My Soul

The Voice That Breathed O'er Eden
The King of Love My Shepherd Is

While the register is being signed

Bach	*Sheep May Safely Graze*
	Jesu Joy of Man's Desiring
Brahms	*Behold a Rose is Blooming*
	How Lovely is Thy Dwelling Place
Handel	*'Minuet' from Berenice*
Schubert	*Ave Maria*

The procession down the aisle

Bach	*Fantasia*
Elgar	*Pomp and Circumstance No.4*
Fletcher	*Festive Toccata*
Harris	*Flourish for an Occasion*
Mendelssohn	*'Wedding March' from A Midsummer Night's Dream*
Parry	*Bridal March*
Purcell	*Trumpet Tune*
Widor	*Toccata*

5

Invitations and Presents

When the wedding is planned with plenty of time to spare, invitations should be sent out six weeks before the date, to maximize the chances of guests being able to accept and to enable the caterers to have final numbers in good time. If the wedding is small and informal, or the time for organizing is strictly limited, then it may not be possible to allow nearly as long, but remember that printing will probably take two to three weeks, so this should be programmed into your schedule. The cheaper and quicker alternative is to buy cards ready-printed from the stationers' and fill in all the details by hand. Once the invitations have gone out, guests will begin enquiring about gifts, so you will need to decide whether you want to circulate a present list (see p.59) or leave them to make their own choice.

Ordering invitations

When calculating the number of invitations needed, remember that children are normally included on their parents' card, though they should be invited separately if they are over eighteen, even if they are still living at home. Invitations should be sent to the best man, bridesmaids and ushers, and even the groom's parents will like one to keep as a souvenir of the day. The minister who performs the ceremony is normally invited, as a courtesy, though he will probably accept only if he knows the couple or their family well. It is always a good idea to order a few more invitations than you think you will need, just in case you have omitted one or two guests you meant to invite.

The stationer will be able to show you a selection of styles and prices and can often advise on the wording if you are in any doubt. Invitations must give the place, the time and the date (though not the year), the location of the reception and the address to which a reply should be sent. As soon as you receive your stationery order, check each detail carefully so that any mistakes can be corrected.

Traditional wording

At most weddings, the bride's parents are hosts and the guests are invited to both the ceremony and the reception, so the formal wording is as follows:

Mr and Mrs Dylan Jones
request the pleasure of the company of

_____

at the marriage of their daughter
Olwen
with
Mr Tristan Smith
at
St Cuthbert's Church, Puckleton
on Saturday, 11th June
at 3 o'clock
and afterwards at the King's Mitre Hotel, Puckleton

R.S.V.P.
Chez Nous
Acacia Avenue
Puckleton

In an alternative form, the name of the person invited is hand-written in the top left hand corner:

Mr and Mrs Dylan Jones
request the pleasure of
your company at the marriage of their daughter
Olwen
to

Mr Tristan Smith
at
St Cuthbert's Church, Puckleton
on Saturday, 11th June
at 3 o'clock
and afterwards at the
King's Mitre Hotel, Puckleton

R.S.V.P.
Chez Nous
Acacia Avenue
Puckleton

When the bride chooses to host the wedding herself, formal invitations read: 'Miss Olwen Jones requests the pleasure of your company at her marriage to Mr Tristan Smith at St Cuthbert's Church, etc.', but if the bride and groom host the wedding jointly, the wording will be 'Mr Tristan Smith and Miss Olwen Jones request the pleasure of your company at their marriage, etc.' Any ranks or titles belonging to either bride or groom should be used: for instance Major and Mrs Dylan Jones, Lt Tristan Smith or Dr Olwen Jones.

On occasions where another relative, rather than the girl's parents, hosts the wedding, then the relationship should be made clear: 'Mr Randolph Jones requests the pleasure of your company at the marriage of his sister Olwen, etc.' or 'Mr and Mrs Piers Plowman request the pleasure of your company at the marriage of their niece Olwen Jones, etc.'

If the groom's parents are arranging and paying for the wedding, perhaps because the bride and her parents are estranged, or the latter are living abroad, the wording might be 'Mr and Mrs Sefton Smith request the pleasure of your company at the marriage of Miss Olwen Jones to their son Tristan, etc.' or 'Mr and Mrs Sefton Smith request the pleasure of your company at the marriage of their son Tristan to Miss Olwen Jones, etc.'

Divorced parents

If a divorced wife is sole host at her daughter's wedding, she uses her own Christian name, not that of her ex-husband, as: 'Mrs

Megan Jones requests the pleasure, etc.' When the divorced couple decide to act as joint hosts, whether the father has remarried or not, the invitations would read 'Mr Dylan Jones and Mrs Megan Jones request the pleasure, etc.' In cases where the wife has remarried, the wording is 'Mr Dylan Jones and Mrs Percival Pickett request the pleasure, etc.'

When the bride's father has married again and he is hosting the wedding along with her stepmother, the invitation could read: 'Mr and Mrs Dylan Jones request the pleasure of your company at the marriage of Mr Jones's daughter Olwen (or simply 'his daughter Olwen') to Mr Tristan Smith, etc.' Similar wording applies in the case of a mother and stepfather, but then the bride's surname may be added for the sake of clarity: 'Mr and Mrs Percival Pickett request the pleasure of your company at the marriage of her daughter Olwen Jones, etc.'

Double weddings

An invitation to the double wedding of two sisters normally reads as follows, with the name of the elder girl coming first:

Mr and Mrs Bertram Bootle
request the pleasure of your company
at the marriage of their daughters
Camilla
with
Mr Henry Hibberd
and
Caroline
with
Mr Christopher Crocker
at St Catherine's Church, etc.

If two couples are hosting a double wedding, as will be the case when brothers or friends, rather than sisters, marry in the same ceremony, the names of both sets of parents will head the invitation and the surname of each bride should be used.

Jewish weddings

The custom in Jewish families is to use the names of both sets of parents on the invitations, as follows:

> Mr and Mrs Benjamin Cohen
> request the pleasure of your company
> at the marriage of their daughter
> Ruth Marian
> to
> David
> son of Mr and Mrs Aaron Samuels, etc.

Second marriages

When a blessing service is arranged to follow a civil marriage, it may be a private service held between the register office ceremony and the reception, but sometimes it is possible to invite guests to the blessing and then to the reception, along the lines:

> Leo White and Lavinia Green
> invite
> . . . .
> to the blessing of their marriage
> at
> St Bartholomew's Church, etc.

When a widow remarries in church, her parents may issue the invitations just as they would for a single daughter, though they would use her married name: 'their daughter Mrs Daniel Green'; alternatively she would send out invitations in her own name, 'Mrs Daniel Green requests, etc.'

Invitations to the reception only

Often, when the ceremony is at a register office, only close family and friends will be present at the ceremony, so the invitations will refer to the reception only. There are two accepted styles among formal invitations, either:

Mr and Mrs William Wilberforce
request the pleasure of your company
at a reception to follow the marriage of their daughter
Samantha
with
Mr Charles Ponsonby
at the Grand Hotel, Kensington
on Saturday 11th June at 1.30 pm

or:

Mr and Mrs William Wilberforce
at home
following the marriage of their daughter
Samantha
to
Mr Charles Ponsonby

R.S.V.P.
45 Bloomingdale Road
Kensington

An 'At Home' does not, strictly speaking, have to take place at the parents' home, but if a hotel is chosen instead, then details have to be given in the same way as the first invitation above.

Invitations to the ceremony only

When, for one reason or another, the bride and groom are marrying in church but not holding a reception, or entertaining only close relatives, they may still wish to invite all their family and friends to the church. The wording can be just as formal as regular invitations – in fact, even more so. The usual form is to 'request the honour of your presence'. Otherwise, the bride and groom can send personal notes to everyone, saying how much they would like to see them in church and explaining that they are not holding a reception but that they hope to give a party once they are settled in their new home.

Informal invitations

These are becoming more and more popular, especially with couples who stage their own weddings. They might read 'Bob and Barbara invite . . . . . . to their marriage at St Stephen's Church, etc.' or perhaps 'Bob Parker and Barbara Butler would like you to come to a party to celebrate their marriage at . . . on . . . ' Of course, the bride's parents may still send the invitations, saying simply, 'Alec and Katie Butler hope that you will join them to celebrate the marriage of Barbara and Bob on . . . at . . . '

Cancelling invitations

In the unfortunate event that a wedding must be cancelled or postponed, perhaps because of death or illness in the family, guests should be notified either by printed card or, if time is short, a handwritten message. In the case of cancellation, this might read:

> Mr and Mrs Dylan Jones regret to announce that owing to the sudden death of the groom's father, the invitations to the marriage of their daughter Olwen with Mr Tristan Smith must be cancelled.

If the wedding is postponed to a later date, the wording might be:

> Mr and Mrs Dylan Jones announce that, owing to the illness of Mrs Jones, they are obliged to postpone the marriage of their daughter Olwen to Mr Tristan Smith which was to have taken place on Saturday, 11th June, to Saturday, 15th September. The time and place remain the same.

Addressing the invitations

The rules of etiquette say that invitations sent to couples are addressed to the wife only but this convention is often ignored and envelopes are addressed to 'Mr and Mrs Sebastian Winter'. If the children in the family are also invited it is a matter of choice whether or not to mention them on the envelope: 'Mr and Mrs Sebastian Winter, Deborah and Dominic.' The minister's invitation is addressed to 'The Reverend Arthur Preach' or 'The Reverend Arthur and Mrs Preach'. In the case of a rabbi, the envelope reads 'The Reverend Rabbi L.Samuels'.

On the invitation itself, any children who are invited should be named so that it reads either 'Mr and Mrs Sebastian Winter, Deborah and Dominic' or 'Sebastian and Annabel, Deborah and Dominic'. When inviting a couple who are living together but are not married, the form can be either 'Mark and Sarah' or 'Mr Mark Musgrave and Miss Sarah Cresswell'. A divorced woman will usually be addressed as 'Mrs Annabel Winter' unless she has reverted to her maiden name, in which case she is addressed in the same way as a single woman. For a widow, it is correct to use either her husband's initials, as in 'Mrs S.L. Winter' or her own first name. The minister's invitations reads as follows: 'Mr Arthur Preach' for the vicar, 'Father Preach' for a Roman Catholic priest and 'Rabbi Samuels' in the Jewish faith.

Replying to invitations

Replies should follow the formality, or informality, of the invitations, so a conventional acceptance will be worded:

> Miss Maisie Higgs has much pleasure in accepting the kind invitation of Mr and Mrs Jones to the marriage of their daughter on Saturday, 11th June at St Cuthbert's Church and afterwards at The King's Mitre Hotel, Puckleton.

A refusal reads:

> Miss Maisie Higgs thanks Mr and Mrs Jones for their kind invitation to the marriage of their daughter Olwen but regrets that she is unable to accept, owing to family commitments.

If one of the recipients accepts and the other declines, it could read:

> Mrs Guy Green has much pleasure in accepting the kind invitation of Mr and Mrs Jones to the marriage of their daughter on Saturday, 11th June at St Cuthbert's Church and afterwards at the King's Mitre Hotel. Mr Green regrets that he is unable to accept as he is abroad on business at the time.

Informal acceptances might read 'Guy and Margaret will be delighted to accept the invitation to your party' or 'Thank you for asking us to come to the church to see you married. We are looking forward to being there, (signed) Guy and Margaret.'

Present lists

Most couples find a sprinkling of white elephants among their wedding gifts – the canary-coloured lampshade or the cushions that seem to be stuffed with stones – but you can cut this to a minimum by making out a detailed present list. There is no need to feel shy about it; those who have their own ideas about gifts will not ask for the list but most will be eager to ensure they are not wasting time and money scouring the shops for something you may not like.

You can keep the list yourself and make two or three suggestions to anyone who enquires, but you are taking the risk that you are asking for something more expensive, or less interesting, than they had in mind. Photocopying a list to send round gives guests the maximum choice but unless you send it to one guest at a time and ask for their decision before sending it to the next person in line, you can end up with a set of duplicates. The half dozen toasters and motley assortment of spice racks are not only disappointingly useless, they are an embarrassment to the senders when they see their carefully chosen gift lined up with its twins in the present display.

One way out is to make two or three separate lists, perhaps one for close relatives who want to make a substantial gift, one for close friends and the rest of the family and another for office friends, fellow students or neighbours, listing smaller, cheaper items. Then if you know that an elderly aunt is ekeing out a small pension you can send her the less expensive list, so that she doesn't feel she is competing with the food mixer or dinner service givers. On the other hand, if a group of people say they want to club together for something sizeable, you can send them the family list. Ask everyone to cross off the gift they have chosen before returning the list.

Some large stores have a special bride's service, so that you can compile your list there. The shop then keeps the list for you and you simply direct friends and relatives there. Guests living out of town can order by phone and be sure of giving a welcome present, and the hesitant can get advice. Then if duplications still occur, you will have no difficulty in exchanging the store items later without hurting anyone's feelings. Another advantage is that the staff can often encourage people to buy, say, a few items of china to make up a set too costly for a single present.

When making your list, especially if you plan to circulate only one, make sure that you include a wide range of items, costing anything from a couple of pounds upwards. There may be no one who wants to give you a pair of oven gloves or a rolling pin, but you should ensure that no guest asks for a list only to find there is nothing they can afford.

Give as much guidance as possible, with your colour schemes firmly in mind. Scarlet towels and purple cushions may look very pretty in the shop and frightful in your carefully decorated home. Even if you are living in a furnished flat to begin with, imagine what colours and styles you will want when you furnish your own home, so that you do not have to replace everything in a few years' time.

When choosing china, it is prudent to pick patterns that are likely to be in stock for some time. If you want something unusual, make sure you have allowed for plenty of spares. Otherwise a couple of breakages can put a whole dinner service out of action.

Most couples concentrate on household items. Linen, china and glass have always been traditional gifts and are still very popular, but if you have had a bachelor flat for several years, or have been married before, you may have most of the basics already. If this is the case, you might prefer to suggest other types of gift: photographic equipment, video cassettes or compact discs, coffee table books, plants for the garden or even a weekend away at a pleasant hotel. They should be items that can be enjoyed by both partners, rather than more personal gifts like jewellery or perfume.

As the gifts arrive, keep a record of who sends what. Inevitably, some will become separated from their gift tags before you write your thank-yous, and you could find yourself thanking someone for a rubbish bin when they actually sent designer place mats.

The following list will serve as a general guideline for your own selection. Remember to specify make, style, colour and number of items, where appropriate.

China and glass
Breakfast set
Dinner service
Tea set

Cutlery
Soup spoons
Table knives and forks
Dessert knives and forks

Coffee set
Fruit dishes
Fruit bowls
Soup bowls
Teapot
Milk jug and sugar basin
Vegetable dishes
Mugs
Egg cups
Butter dishes
Water jug
Sherry glasses
Wine glasses
Tumblers
Liqueur glasses
Brandy glasses
Wine carafe
Decanters
Vases

Dessert spoons
Teaspoons
Serving spoons
Fish knives and forks
Steak knives
Cake forks
Carving sets
Salad servers
Ladles

Kitchen items
Saucepans
Frying pan
Omelette pan
Pressure cooker
Wok
Knives
Knife sharpener
Ovenware
Flan dishes
Ramekins
Baking tins
Carving dish
Set of kitchen
implements
Kitchen scales
Ironing board
Plate rack
Vegetable rack
Bread bin
Storage jars
Spice rack
Chopping board
Bread board and knife
Dish drainer
Wooden spoons

Electrical
Cooker
Dishwasher
Washing machine
Spin drier
Fridge/freezer
Slow cooker
Deep fat fryer
Coffee maker
Kettle
Toaster
Iron
Tea maker
Table lamp
Vacuum cleaner
Food processor
Blender
Coffee grinder
Electric fire
Fan heater
Electric blanket
Clock radio
Radio cassette
Stereo equipment
Video recorder
Tape recorder

Egg whisk
Corkscrew
Rolling pin
Rubbish bin

Television
Home computer

Linen
Sheets
Blankets
Duvet
Pillows
Pillowcases
Bath towels
Hand towels
Tea towels
Bath mat
Tablecloths
Place mats
Napkin
Oven gloves

Miscellaneous
Barbecue
Linen basket
Bathroom scales
Trays
Mirrors
Nest of tables
Magazine rack
Pictures/paintings
Tea trolley
Yogurt maker
Wine rack
Step ladder
Tool kit
Garden tools
Luggage
Clothes drier
House plants
Camera equipment

Thank-you letters

Gifts should be acknowledged promptly, and only those arriving at the very last moment should wait until the return from the honeymoon. The best thank-you letters should give the senders a glow of pleasure, making them feel that the time and money spent on your gift was well worthwhile. Everyone knows that you are writing dozens of similar letters but each one should sound personal, as though you really mean what you say.

Everyone understands that this is a busy time, so you can be brief, but always mention the gift specifically and make some complimentary reference to its appearance or usefulness. The letter might read something like this:

Dear Tom and Fiona,
Hamish and I would like to thank you both for the beautiful lamp. It is such a lovely colour and fits very well with the

colour scheme in our sitting room. It was very kind of you to go to so much trouble to choose something you knew we would enjoy.

We hope that you will come and visit us when we return from honeymoon and see your gift in its new setting!

With best wishes and thanks from us both,

Yours . . . . . .

In the case of money, give some idea of how you plan to spend it, either buying something you need badly for your home or, perhaps, putting it towards the down payment on a house.

Of course, you may find yourselves thanking people for gifts you find neither useful nor decorative. In this case, try to see them through the eyes of the senders and comment on them accordingly: mention the unusual design or colour, the quality of the workmanship or the fact that it will last a lifetime! Never give in to the temptation to joke about a present with comments like 'That colour should certainly wake up our colour scheme' or 'The cookery book looks very comprehensive; are you trying to tell me something about my cooking?' Such remarks may bring a laugh between friends after a drink or two but on paper they can sound offensive.

If you have so many presents that writing to everyone would mean you had no time for essential wedding preparations, you might use printed cards but even then you should add a couple of handwritten lines to each one. Cards are usually worded something like this:

Please accept our sincere thanks for your good wishes and most acceptable gift which has added so much to our happiness.

Sometimes you may receive a present from someone you have not asked to the wedding. This does not mean that you must rush off an invitation – unless, of course, the person has been left off the list by mistake, in which case offer some explanation along with the late invitation. Otherwise, write an appreciative letter and suggest that they join you for coffee or a meal in the near future.

Present displays

Presents are sometimes displayed at the hotel or hall where the reception is held; alternatively they can be set out in a spare room at the bride's home and relatives and friends are invited to see them on one or more evenings, a few days before the wedding. It is often convenient to add a line to thank-you notes, giving a date and time.

Displays are usually mounted on tables covered with white cloths to show off the presents to the best advantage; inverted cardboard boxes can give a tiered effect. Large items can be grouped together on the floor at one end of the room. If you have several lamps or toasters in triplicate, space them out as far as possible, rather than lining them up in rows.

Many couples use the gift tags arriving with the presents to identify the senders when making the arrangement but a white card propped in front of each item, with the name of the sender and, in the case of family, their relationship to the bride and groom, can look neater and is less confusing.

Any item too large for the display should be described on a card placed in a prominent position, for instance 'From Uncle Robert: a grand piano'. Cheques and other financial gifts should be treated in the same way: 'From Mrs Ethel Gold, the bride's grandmother: share certificates' or: 'Cheques received from: Uncle Bert and Aunt Florrie and Uncle Jock'.

Sending a present

Guests invited to a wedding do not *have* to send a present, though this is the usual form. Certainly they should not feel obliged to ask for the bride's present list if they prefer to choose unaided. The gift need not be new: a piece of china from the sender's own collection or an item of Victoriana from an antique shop will be quite suitable, so long as it fits in with the couple's scheme of decoration.

Whenever possible, gifts should be sent in advance rather than taken to the reception, but it is wise to have breakables professionally packed by the store where they were purchased. They are usually addressed to the bride at her home, but friends of the groom, to whom the bride might be a complete stranger, can send their gifts to him. In this case, of course, the thank-you letter is the groom's responsibility.

When writing the accompanying gift card, make sure that you have identified yourself fully. 'With love and best wishes from Carol' may cause difficulties if the bride and groom have half a dozen friends named Carol. The easiest method is to write your full name and address on the reverse of the card.

6

Members of the Wedding

The bride and groom may take the limelight on the big day but a traditional wedding relies for its success on a number of people – the family members who make the arrangements and the attendants who make up the wedding party.

Choosing the attendants

The best man
The bridegroom will normally choose his closest friend as best man. If that friend is reliable, calm, quick-witted and with a good eye for detail, then he is an admirable choice. On the other hand, if he is notoriously absent-minded and always has to fumble through every pocket to find his railway ticket, then perhaps it would be better to choose a relative or a more dependable friend who will not let you down at the wrong moment.

It is not sufficient for the best man to turn up on the day with a carnation in his buttonhole and a smile on his face. He must be the sort of person who can sort things out if the wedding cars go to the wrong address or the church doors are closed and locked because the vicar has muddled the dates. If he has to make a speech, then remember this is a family occasion and avoid the man who is renowned for his *risqué* stories. He must also be someone who can be relied on not to imbibe too freely and end up making a far less suitable speech than was planned — or even no speech at all!

Though choosing the best man has always been the bridegroom's prerogative, it is usual to choose somebody who is reasonably well liked by the bride and acceptable to her family. Though the bride's mother and the bridal couple will probably make all the advance arrangements, the best man can be the chief behind-the-scenes organizer on the day, making sure that nothing is overlooked at the last minute.

At Jewish weddings, the best man is traditionally the bride-groom's eldest brother; otherwise one of the bride's brothers. If neither partner has a brother, the best man is usually another close male relative.

The bridesmaids

Most brides decide on two or four bridesmaids but numbers can range from one to eight. Traditionally, the bride chooses them first from her own sisters, then the sisters of the groom. In practice, many girls choose friends rather than the groom's sisters, who may be near strangers. One tactful way out is to choose equal numbers of bridesmaids from either side of the family and a close friend as chief bridesmaid.

Ideally, the chief bridesmaid should be someone who is good-natured enough to want to put the bride first on her special day and to care just a little more about the bride's appearance than her own. If the arrangements have been made carefully, it is unlikely that there will be any crisis when you have to rely on her but she should be the kind of girl who could cope efficiently if the need arose. In the case of a buffet-style reception, it is an advantage if she is a good mixer.

Bridesmaids are always single girls, so that if your chief attendant is married, she is called a 'matron of honour' and is usually dressed slightly differently from the rest of the bridesmaids. Sometimes it happens that the girl you are thinking of choosing belongs to a different faith; if you have any doubts, take advice from the minister.

Child bridesmaids can look delightful but they do have a habit of running amok at the most awkward moments so it is wise to have at least one adult bridesmaid who can keep an eye on them. If you cannot resist choosing an angelic-looking three-year-old as a flower-girl, make sure that her mother is sitting at the end of the nearest pew, so that she can be rescued if she suddenly bursts into tears as you reach the altar.

Choosing from several small cousins or nieces who all long to be bridesmaids calls for tact. You may shudder at the thought of fat little Marigold, with her pebble glasses and prominent teeth, following you up the aisle, but her mother is unlikely to see it the same way – especially if she has brought Marigold up on the promise that 'When Auntie Amanda gets married, you'll be a bridesmaid'. You might resort to the ploy of matching heights or abandon the idea of child bridesmaids altogether. It would be kind to write to the mothers of children who might have been expecting to be chosen, explaining that you think weddings are too taxing for children of that age, or giving some equally diplomatic explanation.

There is no role for bridesmaids at a register office wedding, but the bride frequently has a female attendant who will hold the flowers if necessary and perhaps acts as witness.

Pageboys

If you plan to include pageboys in your retinue, make sure they are young enough to enjoy the dressing up (probably under eight) and old enough not to howl all the way through the ceremony (four or over). Keep in mind what you know about the children in question: if they normally pull the hair of every little girl within range or shout and yell whenever they get excited, then being kitted out in kilt or velvet knickerbockers is unlikely to change their behaviour.

Ushers

The ushers are the first people your guests meet when they arrive at the wedding, so they should be friendly but dignified. They should also be reliable: not the sort of men to adjourn to the nearest bar for a quick drink before the service, leaving early guests to fend for themselves, or the type who, in times of stress, are likely to be pounding up and down the aisle with scarlet faces and buttonholes askew.

Ushers are usually chosen from among the unmarried friends of both bride and groom. For weddings with fifty guests or less, two ushers are usually needed, with another two for every extra fifty or so.

Role of the best man

The best man's chief duty on the wedding day is to keep the groom calm, smart and prompt. He should be the one producing a spare pair of shoelaces, a clothes brush or an extra clean handkerchief for the groom – not, as happens at some weddings, the other way round. Though he is not officially involved in the wedding preparations he should have a good working knowledge of the arrangements, so that he can discharge his duties properly, leaving the chief participants free to relax and enjoy themselves on the day.

Advance preparations

He may be involved in arranging the stag night, unless the groom prefers to handle this himself, and should certainly make arrangements to see that the groom gets home safely – *by taxi*, if they have both been drinking. At around the same time, he should make sure that the ushers are briefed on their duties, letting them know whether they will be using guest lists for seating in the church, whether they should hand out order of service sheets to each guest at the door or arrange them on the pews beforehand.

The day before the wedding, he can help the groom by checking with the car hire firm that there is no hitch over transport arrangements, if a car has been booked to take the two men to the ceremony. If he is taking the groom in his own car, this is the time for a trip to the car wash, a fill of petrol and a check under the bonnet.

The best man will need to collect morning dress for himself and the bridegroom, if this is being hired. He might also confirm with the florist that the orders for buttonholes are correct and that they will be delivered or collected the next day. He should collect the order of service sheets from the bride's mother and most families will appreciate an offer to help with any fetching and carrying – for instance, helping to transport the presents to the reception venue for display or taking luggage for the bridal couple to the hotel where they will be changing.

If the groom's luggage and going-away clothes have not been taken to the hotel – or the bride's home if the reception is held there – the day before, the best man should allow time to arrange this on the wedding morning. Often an usher or relative can be asked to stand by for this task. Though many men make a detour to drop off the cases on their way to the church, this can turn out to be an irritating distraction and heavy traffic or roadwork can mean a late arrival at the church and panic all round. The best man may also need to allow time to see that the car which the couple will use to start their honeymoon is parked in a convenient place near the reception venue and the keys are safely in his pocket.

The wedding day
The best man should arrive at the groom's home with plenty of time to spare. Apart from helping the bridegroom to dress and making sure he has everything he needs, he will take charge of the wedding ring, putting it safely in a pocket where he keeps nothing else (if he is wearing a waistcoat, this is the ideal place) and also the various travel documents the couple will need for their honeymoon. It is as well to check that passport, tickets, foreign currency, travellers' cheques and hotel confirmations are all present and correct; no one will want to come rushing back in the middle of the reception for a missing document. Usually the church fees will have been settled in advance but sometimes the best man is required to settle the account in the vestry after the service, and he should make sure he has enough spare cash to cover any emergencies. He should also be equipped with a list of taxi firm numbers, just in case any cars break down, before or after the ceremony.

The two men should arrive at church about twenty minutes before the ceremony is due to begin and move to their place facing the altar when the bridesmaids arrive; one of the ushers can be asked to give the signal when this happens. The best man's only part in the ceremony is to produce the ring, immediately after the couple have made their vows, and lay it on the open prayerbook offered by the minister. He escorts the chief bridesmaid to the vestry, where they will probably both be called upon to sign the register as witnesses.

After the photographs, the best man should make sure that the cars leave the church in the right order. He is the last to leave, making sure that no guests are left stranded in the churchyard, so he must make sure that a car is reserved to take him to the reception. If he is using his own car, someone should be on hand to drive it. Parking space is sure to be limited by the time he arrives at the reception and no best man should go missing for half an hour while he drives around looking for a parking space.

If there are speeches, the best man may be called upon to act as toastmaster, calling for order when the meal is over and calling on the first speaker to propose the toast to the bride and bridegroom. Later in the proceedings, he responds to the toast to the bridesmaids, keeping his remarks reasonably brief, unless he is renowned as a good public speaker. He also reads out any telemessages, keeping them so that the couple can reply to them later. If the reception includes dancing, he should dance with the bride, both mothers and the bridesmaids.

When the couple leave the reception to change into their going-away clothes, he must see that the honeymoon luggage is ready and, if the couple are leaving in their own car, that it is securely locked into the boot. A good friend will see that merry guests are not able to do anything more serious than attach the odd streamer or string of tin cans to the car. Once the bridegroom has changed he will hand over the car keys and honeymoon documents.

Once the couple have left, the best man collects the groom's wedding clothes; later he will return any hired finery. He should be among the last of the bridal party to leave, making a last-minute check to make sure that no toppers, umbrellas or gloves have been left behind and, if necessary, helping the bride's parents to remove wedding presents from the display and store them safely.

Role of the bridesmaids

The chief bridesmaid often stays overnight with the bride, or arrives in good time on the wedding morning so that she can help the bride with hair, dress and makeup, unless the bride's mother prefers to fill this role. She can also help the bride's mother to iron out any last-minute hitches in the arrangements, make sure that the right number of bouquets arrive in good time and help to dress child attendants.

The bridesmaids travel to the church ahead of the bride and wait for her there. The chief bridesmaid has the task of checking that nothing is amiss with the attendants' clothes and that they all have the right flowers.

When the bride arrives, the chief bridesmaid will adjust her train and veil, paying particular attention to the view from the back and checking that all fastenings are secure. Then she arranges the attendants in the chosen order, ready for the procession up the aisle.

As the procession reaches the altar, the chief bridesmaid should be ready to take the bride's bouquet, prayerbook or whatever else she is carrying, so that her hands are free to receive the ring. If necessary, she will lift the bride's veil from her face and arrange it neatly, either before the minister begins the service or in time for the couple to take their vows. She must be sure to take the bouquet into the vestry when the couple go to sign the register, so that the bride can carry it in the procession down the aisle. All that the other bridesmaids are required to do is look decorative and dignified.

The bridesmaids have no specific duties at the reception but they can contribute towards everyone's enjoyment by keeping an eye on younger guests, as well as elderly relatives who may need a little help. The chief bridesmaid may be called upon to help the bride to change and it is her job to take charge of the wedding dress and accessories, make sure that arrangements are made for their safe-keeping and check that nothing is left behind.

Role of the ushers

The ushers should arrive at the ceremony at least half an hour before the ceremony – forty-five minutes would be better. They should greet each guest, asking if he or she is a friend of the bride or groom, then show them to their places for the service. The bride's relatives and friends sit in the pews on the left of the nave facing the altar, those of the groom sit in the pews on the right. They should also make sure that each guest has an order of service leaflet or hymn sheet.

At a large, formal wedding the ushers may have a list of guests, so that close family can be shown to the front pews, with relatives in the seats behind them and friends further back. If there are no lists and the numbers are too uneven, perhaps because the bride has lived abroad or the bridegroom's relatives are in the midst of a family feud, then the ushers can even things up tactfully. The head usher should know the bride's mother by sight, so that he can escort her to the right seat.

Once everyone is seated the ushers should take their places at the back, so that they can look after any latecomers. After the ceremony, they should help the best man to arrange transport for guests without cars.

Role of the bride's mother

The bride's mother is chiefly concerned with planning and preparation, in conjunction with her daughter. It is traditionally her responsibility to deal with the wedding announcements, compile the guest list, send out the invitations, make the reception arrangements, order flowers, cars and photographer. In practice, the chores will probably be shared by the bridal couple – and, of course, by her husband.

Wedding guests who are travelling a long distance may need overnight accommodation. Sometimes the bride's parents put them up, but remember that the wedding day is a busy enough time without having to worry about house guests. It might be more practical to offer to book accommodation for them, but this would normally be at their own expense, so make this clear by mentioning the price when you give them details.

On the wedding morning some mothers like to help their daughters to dress; others prefer to leave it to the chief bridesmaid. At the appointed time the bride's mother will leave for the church, either with the bridesmaids or in the second car, leaving the bride to follow with her father. It is a good idea to take along a 'repair' kit – safety pins, needle and cotton, tissues, a spare pair of tights – as the bride will have nowhere to carry such emergency extras.

At the reception the bride's mother is hostess (unless the whole wedding has been organized by the bride and groom), so she will want to make sure that no one stands alone in a corner and that each guest has a few words with the bride and groom. Even if there is no receiving line, the bride's parents should be at the door to greet everyone as they arrive. If the reception takes the form of a formal wedding breakfast, she will judge the right moment – when everyone has been greeted and served with drinks – to give the signal for the bride and groom to take their seats at the top table so that the meal can begin.

After the wedding she may see that slices of wedding cake are boxed and sent to those unable to attend the wedding, as well as circulating wedding photographs to those who might wish to order prints.

Role of the bride's father

The bride's father may or may not be involved in the wedding preparations, though his role will depend to some extent on whether he is paying for all or part of the celebrations. On the day itself he will escort his daughter to church and lead the procession to the altar with the bride on his right arm.

When the minister asks, 'Who gives this woman to be married to this man?' he takes the bride's right hand and gives it to the minister. There is no provision for a response in the Church of England service, so he need not say anything, but if he feels foolish standing silent, a murmured 'I do' is in order. He should decide in advance which suits him better, as an occasional father has been known to pipe up eagerly in the heat of the moment, 'Me!'

At the reception the bride's father may give a short speech, proposing the toast to the bride and groom, but if he dreads the idea of public speaking, feels embarrassed at extolling the virtues of his own daughter or would simply prefer to enjoy the reception without the thought of a speech hanging over him, the toast may be proposed by another male relative or an old friend of the family.

If the bride's parents are divorced, she may want her father to give her away or, if the separation was many years ago and she has been brought up by a stepfather, the latter may perform that function. It is the bride's choice, and the rest of those involved need to suspend any hard feelings for the duration of her special day. However, if the bride is marrying from her mother's house and relations between her parents are strained, it is best if her father times his arrival to coincide as nearly as possible with his ex-wife's departure for the church.

At the church, the seating arrangements are slightly different for divorced or separated parents. In this case the bride's mother will sit in the first pew, either with her second husband or a male relative as escort, and the bride's father in the second pew, with his second wife if he has remarried.

Role of the groom's parents

The bridegroom's parents have no traditional role in the wedding preparations, though families now often tend to share duties and costs rather more evenly. Where the bride's parents are living at the other end of the country and the couple are marrying in the groom's home town, his parents may take on most of the arrangements usually handled by the bride's family.

On the wedding day itself, the groom's parents can help most by shelving any differences they may have with their future daughter-in-law or her family, by mixing well and making sure that guests from their side of the family are introduced all round and that no one feels neglected.

The rehearsal

A rehearsal is not essential, except for a large formal wedding, but the bridal party may feel happier if they know exactly what they are supposed to be doing. Ministers of Free Churches often prefer to hold a rehearsal, especially if the church has no centre aisle, so that everyone can be sure of their movements.

It can take place up to a week before the ceremony and the bride and groom, best man, bridesmaids and the bride's father need to be there. The bride's mother and the groom's parent may also attend. It is helpful if the bridesmaids carry mock bouquets and, if the bride plans to wear a train, she should practise with a similar length of material.

The usual order of procession to the altar is as follows:

Minister

Groom   Best man

Bride's Father   Bride

Child Bridesmaid

Chief Bridesmaid

Bridesmaid

The chief bridesmaid and second bridesmaid could walk together, or form the first pair if there are an even number of adult bridesmaids.

The bridal party at a Roman Catholic wedding may follow the same pattern, or the groom, as well as the best man and bridesmaids, may wait for the bride at the church door. The priest then leads the procession up the aisle, as follows:

Priest

Bride and Groom

Best Man and Chief Bridesmaid

Bridesmaids

Bride's parents
Bridegroom's parents

Gifts for the attendants

It is usual for the bridegroom to give presents to the best man and bridesmaids, as a thank-you for their contribution to the pleasure of the day. These can be given before the ceremony or during the reception.

Gifts for the adult attendants usually take the form of personal keepsakes. For the bridesmaids the popular choice is jewellery, given in time to be worn during the ceremony – perhaps earrings, a bracelet or a cross on a chain, a brooch or pendant with the girl's birthstone or a pretty watch. Possible alternatives are a personalized pen set, a compact or an evening bag.

The best man may be given cuff-links, a watch, a lighter, an engraved tankard or brandy goblet. However, if these gifts would be mere white elephants to your best man, it is better to forget the conventional choices and buy something more in keeping with his interests and life-style: a personal organizer, a computer software package, even a set of darts!

Child bridesmaids are often given jewellery but, depending on their age, a toy might be more suitable, and will usually be the best choice for pageboys. An electronic game will probably keep them happily occupied during the reception. For a girl, a bride doll, or a small doll dressed in a replica of her bridesmaid's outfit, will be a happy reminder. Other possibilities include a simple camera or radio. Gifts of premium bonds or savings certificates may be appreciated by parents, but children usually prefer something they can put to good use right away.

Gifts for parents

Some couples like to give their parents a gift, to thank them for their contribution to the success of the wedding and, indeed, for making the whole thing possible in the first place. Possible choices are flowers chosen to echo the colours of the bridal bouquets, a silver-framed wedding photo, an engraved flower bowl or vase – or, perhaps, a rose-bush or flowering tree for the garden, or a bottle of champagne and two glasses, so that they can hold a private celebration while the bridal pair are on honeymoon.

The guests

Guests always answer wedding invitations in writing, whether they are able to accept or not. If they will not be at the wedding, they may like to send a telemessage, which should be sent to the home of the bride or direct to the reception venue.

Guests are not expected to follow the bridal party into morning dress, but it is a good idea to check on the style of the wedding (i.e. formal or informal) before deciding how to dress. Open-necked shirt and sandals would not be appropriate for a wedding where the groom is resplendent in tails and topper. It is no longer essential for women to cover their heads for church weddings, though many will prefer to wear hats, but at a Jewish wedding both men and women are expected to keep their heads covered.

Ten minutes before the start of the ceremony is a good time to arrive, and after the ceremony, guests wait until the bridal party and their immediate family have left the church first. At the reception, too, guests are expected to stay until the bride and groom have left. If you must go before that, then you should leave as unobtrusively as possible.

Surprisingly, formal 'thank-you' notes are not expected after a wedding but any hostess, whether the bride or her mother, will be pleased with a personal note saying how much you enjoyed the day.

Personal checklists

The allocation of responsibilities will vary from one family to another. Use the following specimen lists to make your own checklist as a memory jogger.

Bride's mother
Before the wedding day
Make the guest list
Make reception arrangements
Send out invitations
Keep list of acceptances and refusals
Order cake, flowers, photographer, wedding cars
Arrange own outfit/ liaise with groom's mother
Help bride with her dress and bridesmaids' dresses
Draw up seating plan for church and reception, if necessary
Fix any necessary accommodation for guests
Arrange gift display

On the day
Check that the right flowers arrive on time
Help the bride to dress
Take emergency repair kit
Leave for church in time to arrive 10 minutes before the ceremony
Receive guests formally or informally
Give the signal for the meal to begin
Ensure that all the guests have the opportunity to talk to the bride and groom

After the wedding
Send out cake to absent guests
Circulate photos and collect orders
Insert wedding announcement in a newspaper

Bride's father
Before the wedding:
Arrange own wedding outfit
Write speech
Keep record of bills and pay promptly

On the day:
Escort the bride to church so that the ceremony begins on time
Give the bride away
Greet guests formally or informally
Propose the toast to the bride and groom

Best man
Before the wedding:
Arrange stag night, if necessary
Arrange own wedding outfit
Send wedding present
Brief ushers
Write speech
Check arrangements for cars, flowers, etc
Collect order of service sheets

On the day:
Take honeymoon luggage and going-away clothes to reception venue
Collect buttonholes, if necessary
Take charge of ring
Take charge of honeymoon travel documents
Help groom to dress
See that groom gets to church in good time
Give ring to bridegroom at appropriate moment
Check that the church fees have been paid; pay them in vestry, if necessary
Make sure all guests have transport to the reception
Arrange for going-away car to be conveniently parked
Make speech replying to toast to the bridesmaids
See that honeymoon luggage is in the car
Return honeymoon travel documents to groom
Take charge of groom's wedding clothes

Chief bridesmaid
Before the wedding:
Arrange own outfit
Send wedding present

On the day:
Help bride to dress, if necessary
Check on young attendants' appearances
Arrange bride's dress and veil
Take bride's bouquet
Lift bride's veil
Return bouquet to bride in vestry
Help with younger guests at reception
Help bride to change

Ushers
Before the wedding
Arrange own wedding outfit
Send wedding present
Liaise with best man on arrangements
Collect order of service sheets from best man

On the day:
Hand out order of service sheets
Show guests to seats in church
Escort bride's mother to seat
Help ensure all guests have transport to reception

7

Planning the Reception

In most cases style of the reception will fit in with the style of the whole day, with a large morning dress wedding followed by a formal 'wedding breakfast' or an elegant buffet in a hotel banqueting room, and a small, no-fuss ceremony by an informal party at home, the pub or perhaps a local hall. There are, however, no rules. There are many reasons why a couple might want a private ceremony, whether religious or civil, and there is no reason why they should not follow this with a sumptuous meal for 200, followed by dancing and live entertainment and champagne flowing well into the night.

The trouble-free way to organize a reception is, of course, to turn the whole thing over to the experts and have them lay on everything. Unfortunately, this can be extremely expensive, and cutting the costs to fit into a limited budget can mean taking on a good deal of work and worry.

Booking a hotel

Hotels have a great deal to recommend them as reception venues. The rooms are usually large and well-decorated, the staff experienced in organizing functions, and the facilities (kitchen, car parks, loos) designed to cater for large numbers.

Unless you have your heart set on a particular hotel, try three or four to get an idea of comparative prices and facilities. Take a careful, unhurried look around the hotel, talk to the staff and sample the food. Note whether the staff are efficient and friendly, and whether the rooms you are offered for the reception are attractive and spacious enough but not so large that your guests will be lost in them. Access to a garden can be a big plus for a summer wedding. When you look at menus and consider estimates, remember to check on the following:

○ Does the estimate cover catering only or is the cost of the reception room included?

○ Are VAT and service included?

○ Are tips normally expected in addition to a service charge?

○ Are flowers included?

○ Can the hotel provide a toastmaster, and what will this cost?

○ Do you have to pay extra for cloakroom staff?

○ Is there a time limit on your use of the rooms?

○ Does the package include a changing room for the bride and groom, and is there any discount for staying overnight?

Remember that the best hotel is the one that sends its customer away happy and satisfied. In most towns, it is easy enough to find other couples who have held a wedding reception there. Ask if they felt that they had value for money and if there were any minor failures that could be ironed out by a word with the banqueting manager in advance.

Hall or home

A reception at home can be intimate and welcoming, as well as far less costly than a hotel. However, it can entail an enormous amount of extra work and last-minute upheaval. It also limits the number of guests; the average house will hold about thirty people in reasonable comfort; a large house will manage fifty. Though guests can spill over into the garden on a fine day, it would be foolish to count on good weather, even in summer. You will also have to take into account the car-parking space in the locality; it will not add to the party spirit if half the guests are worrying about cars that have been left double parked or on yellow lines.

If the numbers on your guest list are far greater than the capacity of your home, you might think about hiring a marquee, which can make a romantic summer venue. However, you need a very large garden to accommodate a marquee and you need to think carefully about the number of available loos and, in the event of rain, whether your guests will have to negotiate a wet and boggy expanse of lawn in getting to and from the marquee. When considering a marquee, make sure you see a picture of what it will look like when erected and ask the hirer to inspect the site to make sure it is suitable. Ask about coloured linings to fit in with your overall scheme. You will also need lighting, tables and chairs and perhaps a floor to stop feet sinking into the lawn, so shop around for all-in prices.

Hiring a hall allows for a large reception, with the option of a sit-down meal, but, if you are doing your own catering, there will be many journeys to and fro to add to the work, and if you hire outside caterers the saving on hotel prices may not be as substantial as you had hoped. Halls often have very limited cooking facilities and can be very drab and depressing, needing many hours of work to make them attractive enough for a reception. If you are thinking of booking a hall, take the following into account:

○ Are there enough tables and chairs or will you need to hire more?

○ Is there an extra charge if you use the kitchen?

○ Are the kitchen facilities sufficient for your needs: will it be possible to heat food on the premises; will you be able to make tea and coffee?

○ Are the cloakroom facilities adequate?

○ Will the wedding cars be able to draw up outside without difficulty?

○ Is there a charge for corkage if you provide your own wine? (Some local authorities have agreements with caterers who either provide the drinks or charge on every bottle you open.)

○ Are there any restrictions on alcohol or smoking?

○ At what time will you be able to have access to the hall to begin preparations?

○ At what time must you vacate the hall?

○ What are the insurance arrangements?

○ Will the caretaker make sure that the rooms are clean and tidy for your arrival?

A different venue

Apart from the usual hotels and halls, there are many other

possibilities for a wedding reception. A party on the water can be very pleasant on a summer afternoon and if you live near a river or canal, there are sure to be firms offering the hire of boats, with or without a whole catering package (consult Yellow Pages). Some hotels and leisure centres can lay on a pool-side party, with a charge per head for catering, plus a fee for the hire of the pool for a specified period.

A number of stately homes take bookings for wedding receptions, so that you can receive your guests in imposing marble halls or panelled dining rooms. (Ask at National Trust regional offices or the nearest stately home.)

Wedding receptions have been held in breweries, on board charter planes, in mock medieval banqueting halls, on board double-decker buses or illuminated trams on Blackpool sea front. It only takes imagination, organization – and money.

Engaging a caterer

Whether you are hiring a hall or marquee or holding the party at home, you may want to engage a catering firm to provide and serve the food. Standards and prices vary wildly so it is wise to ask around for personal recommendations. If you do need to hire a firm without a recommendation, find out how long they have been in business and ask them for details of other weddings where they have handled the catering. If they are not familiar with the venue you have chosen, ask for someone to visit the site with you and ensure that the meal you want can be served there without difficulty. Notice how your initial enquiries are received: efficiency and attention to detail in the early stages are a good indication of the final results. Compare menus and prices from several rival firms and make sure you check the following:

o Does the price include providing glasses, crockery, linen, etc?
o Are tea and coffee included?
o How many people will be serving?
o Is hot food included and if so, what are the arrangements for heating and keeping it hot?
o Are they able to provide a toastmaster and cloakroom staff, if required?
o Will they clear up afterwards at no extra cost?

○ Are VAT, service and insurance included?

○ Are tips normally expected in addition?

○ What time will they arrive to begin work?

Some catering services are run by women from home, with the help of their friends and family, and though they are sometimes very good, they may not have the professional expertise or the back-up services available to an established firm. If you book with this type of caterer, make sure that adequate arrangements can be made if she falls ill the week before the wedding.

Self-catering

Only those with a flair for organizing and plenty of willing and reliable friends and relatives should attempt to cater for a large wedding reception, and even a small family wedding will need meticulous advance planning. Most of the food will be prepared in advance and frozen, so make sure that you have promises of sufficient freezer space from friends before the preparations begin. Remember that food will have to come out of the freezer in the last couple of days and then be kept cool, so make sure, at the same time, that enough refrigerator space is available. Never rely on Auntie May and Mrs Jones down the street who vaguely promise to contribute 'a little something'. You will need to be ruthless about pinning everyone down, so that you know where every quiche is coming from. Make careful lists of everyone who will help on the day: who will prepare the room, who will lay out the food and add the finishing touches, who will help to serve, who will pour the drinks, who will clear up afterwards.

If you have gaps in your list of helpers or are unwilling to ask enough people to work instead of enjoying the party, you might consider hiring waiters and waitresses to serve food prepared by friends and family. The manager of a local hotel or the catering school in the nearest city may be able to advise; otherwise try agencies listed in the Yellow Pages. You will usually need one waiter for every fifteen guests unless the staff are very experienced. On the day, make sure that they arrive well in advance so that you (or a member of your family) can brief them over a drink, perhaps asking them to make sure that older members of the party are well looked after, telling them how often to take round the drinks and which foods are in plentiful or short supply. Gratuities given before the party, rather than afterwards, can oil the wheels.

For a small party, you might be able to collect up enough crockery and linen from friends and neighbours. Otherwise you will need to hire them. The names of firms who hire out every possible thing you might need can be found in the Yellow Pages. Make a checklist of the items you will need, and the amount of each, along these lines:

Dinner knives and forks
Dessert spoons
Cake forks
Teaspoons
Dinner plates, tea plates
Dishes
Serving plates, dishes and bowls
Cups and saucers
Glasses
Linen: tablecloths, napkins
Tables, chairs
Cake stand and knife
Bottle openers and corkscrews
Ashtrays
Wastepaper baskets

When ordering from a hire firm, check the position on delivery and collection, insurance and breakages.

The seating plan

At a seated meal, the main bridal party usually sit at the top table, facing the guests. The bride and groom sit in the centre, with the bride on the groom's left, and the bride's parents, as hosts, on either side of them. The usual layout is:

```
Best man
Groom's mother
Bride's father
Bride
Bridegroom
Bride's mother
Groom's father
Chief bridesmaid
```

Strictly speaking, married couples should not sit next to one another at table but if there are strains between the two families it might be best, in the interests of a happy day, to seat them as follows:

```
Best man
Groom's father
Groom's mother
Bride
Bridegroom
Bride's mother
Bride's father
Chief bridesmaid
```

If the parents of either bride or groom are divorced and remarried, their partners normally join the top table but this does not affect the positions on either side of the bridal couple:

```
Bride's stepmother
Best man
Groom's mother
Bride's father
Bride
Groom
Bride's mother
Groom's father
Chief bridesmaid
Groom's stepfather
```

It is usual to draw up a seating plan for the rest of the guests and arrange place cards on the tables. Though there is nothing to stop you inviting the guests to sit wherever they wish, it can result in confusion, with odd places left here and there and people wandering around looking bewildered. If you prefer to give them this freedom, then an arrangement of small tables for four to six people might be a better idea.

When making your plan you may prefer to have the bride's relations down one side of the room and the groom's down the other, or alternate them so that they will get to know one another. You might want to mix the age groups, though it is probably more successful socially to group your friends together, rather than dotting them among the aunts and uncles.

Bear in mind what you know about your guests: it would be tactless to seat relatives who have not spoken for ten years side by side or to put a now-married friend next to a previous fiancé

The food

Hotel and catering firms will have a selection of menus and, if they are doing their job properly, will be able to advise you on the right choice for the type of reception you prefer. If you are providing a sit-down meal then everyone will be eating basically the same food, so it is wise not to be too adventurous. It is better to stick to safe choices like chicken or roast meat and ensure that the quality is high, rather than picking something more exotic and finding that the oldest and the youngest in your party cannot eat it.

If you are doing the catering yourself, a buffet is usually more practical, but remember that dishes like risotto, a chicken mayonnaise or fish mousse take far less time to prepare than scores of little 'nibbles'. The test for food at a stand-up buffet is whether it can be eaten easily with a fork. A table beautifully set out with joints of beef and ham looks splendid but the food is impossible to eat when you are balancing a glass in one hand and a plate in the other. At a buffet guests can select for themselves so you can, if you wish, provide more elaborate food, but make sure that none of your choices are likely to fall to pieces as soon as they are handled, or drip down the front of your guests' best clothes.

The buffet table will look best if you arrange foods of contrasting colours alongside one another. Organize the layout so that guests work their way along from one end of a long table to the other. This sequence is usually satisfactory: plates, salads, fish, meat, vegetables, bread and other accompaniments, cutlery.

At a lunchtime or early afternoon reception, guests who have travelled a long way and missed their elevenses will expect a filling repast. If you have to manage with very little help, then a midday or early evening drinks party with chicken drumsticks, sausages and cheese cubes on sticks or a paté and wine party might fit the bill. A budget alternative is a mid-afternoon reception with sandwiches and little cakes, served with tea or coffee, with champagne only for the toasts. The main drawback here is that dainty sandwiches take a long time to prepare and need to be fresh, so you need willing helpers on the day.

Choose food for your reception with an eye to the season. Your guests will not enjoy sweltering through two or three hot courses in high summer, or wading through the snow to salad and ice cream. On the other hand, you can never count on a July heatwave and one hot choice on the buffet menu can be very welcome on a rainy day in a chilly tent.

The cake

Cakes come in all shapes and sizes: round or square, with or without tiers and pillars, shaped as hearts, lovers' knots or lucky horseshoes. In Britain the traditional type is a rich fruit cake with white royal icing, though more and more brides are now choosing colours to tone with the flowers in their bouquet or with the bridesmaids' dresses – cream, pale blue, lemon or pink. When choosing the style of cake, keep in mind the reception venue and the bride's appearance: a towering, multi-layered cake may look very impressive in the brochure but it needs a high-ceilinged room and a tall bride if it is to look impressive at the wedding.

Thick royal icing can be very hard, so it can be a good idea to have a cut made through the icing, ready for the bride and groom to insert the knife and cut the first slice. Make sure that the caterers, or whoever is dealing with the cake at the reception, know how much you will need in reserve, in order to send small slices to guests who were unable to accept your invitation, and whether or not you want to follow the tradition of saving a tier for the christening.

If the conventional type of cake is not to your taste, there is no reason why you should not choose something different. You might prefer a sponge cake with pretty frosting and light decorations, or a handsome iced chocolate cake, or a pyramid of profiteroles bound together with spun sugar, as offered by a fashionable London store.

The drinks

The first drink offered at a reception is usually sherry, served to guests as soon as they pass down the receiving line. At a large wedding where guests may have to wait for some time for their turn, the sherry (or wine if you prefer) may be served as they arrive but it can mean that people are juggling handbags and glasses as they try to shake hands.

Champagne is, of course, the traditional wedding drink but you do not have to serve it. In fact, you do not have to serve alcohol; some religious faiths ban it altogether and still manage to have an enjoyable reception with soft drinks and juices or, perhaps, an exotic fruit cup. At a drinks party with light refreshments, champagne may be served all the way through or a sparkling wine such as the Italian *spumante* or French *mousseux* might be substituted. These are less expensive and make a light, refreshing accompaniment to buffet food.

If still wine is served with a buffet, white or rosé is probably the best choice as it goes down well with a wide range of foods, from chicken to wedding cake. For a sit-down meal, the wine will be chosen according to the menu, or you might offer a choice of red or white. For either style of reception, you might want to serve guests with a glass of sparkling wine for the toasts.

For a winter wedding, a hot punch made from spiced red wine can be very acceptable and if you find yourselves marrying in a 'cold snap', you could provide rum and Coke or whisky and ginger as a warming first round. In hot weather, order extra soft drinks and think about providing iced coffee as an alternative to hot beverages at the end of the meal.

Whatever your chosen drinks, order from the wine merchant on a sale or return basis so that you can be sure of having enough, without paying for far more than you need. Calculate on the basis of at least half a bottle of wine to each guest (guests at sit-down meals always consume more than those at a buffet) and six glasses of champagne or sparkling wine to a bottle. If a hotel is providing the drinks, make sure that they are charging only for the bottles actually opened.

At an evening party, or a midday reception in a public house, it is quite usual to have a 'cash bar' where you pay for the first couple of rounds and provide wine for the toasts but otherwise guests pay for their own drinks.

Toastmasters

At large formal weddings, a toastmaster usually comes as part of the package and most hotels and catering firms can provide one, if asked. A toastmaster can contribute greatly to the smooth running of the reception, beginning his duties by announcing each of the guests as they arrive and move towards the receiving line. He will then call the guests to their seats when the meal is about to be served. He announces the person who is to say grace and then, at the coffee stage, calls for order when the time comes to cut the cake. He formally calls upon each of the speakers to propose the toasts. Later he will announce the imminent departure of the bride and groom.

It is quite easy to arrange for your own toastmaster, without going to the expense of hiring a professional. The best man, the bride's uncle, the groom's father or one of the guests can fulfil the task. All he needs is a resounding voice and a confident manner. Each time he needs to make an announcement, he will bang the table three times for silence.

The flowers

Flowers add an air of elegance and luxury to the reception venue, whether it is a hotel ballroom or a boat. The decorations may be in the hands of the hotel or catering firm, in which case you should discuss the best sites and types of arrangements with them, or you may prefer to arrange your own. The colours should echo those in the dresses and bouquets of the bridal party and the flowers should be positioned where they will make the most impact.

The key position is usually near the entrance, where the bride and groom will be receiving their guests, and, as everyone will be standing at this point, they must be at eye level. If you are holding the reception at home, a profusion of flowers in the porch, or garlands down the staircase with a matching arrangement below, makes a great impression. Marquees can be decorated with hanging baskets and flowers twined round the supporting poles.

Table decorations need a great deal of thought. At a buffet meal they tend to get in the way; tall arrangements in the corners of the room – or as a focal point on the mantelpiece in a private house – may be more suitable. At a sit-down meal, never place tall arrangements on the top table, so that the bridal couple are obscured from view. A better answer is a low arrangement along the front of the table, with flowers flowing over the edge, or garlands along the front to break up the huge expanse of white cloth. Any flower arrangements on the other tables should be low and spreading so that guests can see one another without craning their necks. When the cake stands on a separate table the bouquets are usually arranged round it.

Remember that it is not always necessary to spend a lot of money on flowers that will have withered by the following day. Some florists will hire out potted plants and it is possible to buy pretty garlands of artificial flowers.

Extra hints for a happy reception

○ The seating plan should be made out clearly and pinned up where everyone can see it, but keep it well clear of the entrance to avoid a bottle-neck.

○ Some of the guests may be vegetarians or vegans, or allergic to fish, or may only eat kosher food, so check in advance and make sure that the menu contains something they can eat.

○ Everyone should be able to see the bridal couple without having to twist their heads round, so arrange the tables accordingly: parallel rows mean that half the guests will be unable to see the top table.

○ The bride and groom should not be half hidden behind the wedding cake; if the top table is narrow, stand the cake on a separate table so that everyone can admire it – and the bride.

○ Highchairs should be provided for the very young and small children will appreciate cushions to enable them to reach the table comfortably.

○ Even at a buffet reception, elderly and infirm guests will need seats; position these near the buffet table.

○ Anyone organizing a reception at home would be well advised to hire druggets to protect the carpets from scattered canapés and spilled wine.

○ There should always be a good supply of soft drinks for children and teetotallers.

○ Wedding cakes are fragile, so the bride and groom should be careful not to lean on the cake as they try to cut through the knife resistant icing. Cakes have been known to topple and crash to the floor.

○ If the bride and groom are setting off on a honeymoon journey, the caterers for a buffet reception can be asked to make up a small pack of goodies to add to their luggage. The bridal couple often find that they eat very little at their own reception.

8

The Wedding Day

This is the day everyone has been waiting for, the day that will prove all the planning and effort well worthwhile. It is not a day to be late, even by ten minutes. The ceremony should begin right on time and the rest of the celebrations should follow on schedule. (See Chapter 10, p.124, for suggested timetable.)

The Church of England ceremony

As soon as the bridal procession is ready, the organist strikes up the first chord of the wedding music and the congregation rise to their feet. The bridegroom and best man step forward into the aisle to stand facing the altar, the best man on the right. The groom should turn to greet the bride as she arrives on the arm of her father. As the procession comes to a halt, the chief bridesmaid takes the bride's bouquet and, if necessary, lifts her veil. The positions for the ceremony are as follows:

Altar

Minister

Bride   Bridegroom

Bride's father   Best Man

Chief Bridesmaid

Bridesmaids

The service may begin with a hymn or with a prayer and bible reading. The minister will then read from the prayerbook, explaining the reasons for marriage and its Christian significance. He then asks if anyone knows of any impediment to the marriage. Providing no one voices an objection, the marriage can continue.

The minister asks the bridegroom:

> Wilt thou have this woman to thy wedded wife, to live together according to God's law in the holy estate of matrimony? Wilt thou love her, comfort her, honour and keep her in sickness and in health and, forsaking all other, keep thee only unto her, so long as ye both shall live?

The bridegroom answers, 'I will'. The minister asks the bride to consent to the same obligations and she, too, answers, 'I will'.

The minister asks, 'Who giveth this woman to be married to this man?' and the bride's father, who is not required to say anything, takes the bride's right hand and gives it to the minister. Once he has performed this duty, the bride's father may retire to the front pew to sit with his wife, or remain in his place until after the couple have been pronounced man and wife.

There are several versions of the marriage ceremony and if the minister is following the version from the Alternative Service Book, 1980, the wording will be simpler and more modern and the giving away ceremony will be omitted. Many couples prefer this, taking the view that marriage is an equal partnership, so that the idea of giving away the bride is outdated. It might also be omitted if the bride's father is dead or absent, though it is accepted form for another male relative, or an old family friend, to take over. There is no rule that the 'giver' must be male: the bride could walk up the aisle without an escort and her mother could step forward to give her away.

The bridegroom then repeats his vows, prompted by the minister, and the bride follows suit:

> I . . . take thee . . . to my wedded wife/husband, to have and to hold from this day forward, for better for worse, for richer for poorer, in sickness and in health, to love and to cherish, till death us do part, according to God's holy law, and thereto I give thee my troth.

The vows are almost the same in the various versions of the service, though the bride may choose to include the word 'obey' after 'to love and to cherish' and the Alternative Services version has 'wife' instead of 'wedded wife' and 'this is my solemn vow' instead of the final sentence.

Immediately after the vows, the best man produces the ring and lays it on the open prayerbook held by the minister. After blessing the ring, the minister offers it to the bridegroom, who puts it on the ~~fourth~~ finger of the bride's left hand and holds it there while he repeats after the minister:

3rd

> With this ring I thee wed, with my body I thee honour and all my worldly goods with thee I share. In the name of the Father and of the Son and of the Holy Ghost.

Once again the modernized words of the alternative service differ slightly, but the same sentiments are expressed. If both partners are receiving a ring, the bride receives her ring first, then puts the ring on the groom's finger. In the alternative version, the bride repeats similar words to those of the groom. The couple are then pronounced man and wife.

Following the blessing and prayers, the minister leads the way to the vestry followed by the bride and groom, then the best man and the chief bridesmaid and both sets of parents. Bride and groom both sign the register, together with the best man and bridesmaid as witnesses. As the organ strikes up for the recessional, the order of the procession down the aisle is as follows:

Altar

Bride's Father   Groom's Mother

Groom's Father   Bride's Mother

Bridesmaids

Best Man   Chief Bridesmaid

Groom   Bride

If the photographer is taking pictures of the bride and groom as they leave the church, the best man and bridesmaid should stop and the whole procession come to a halt until this has been done.

The Roman Catholic ceremony

There are two forms of Roman Catholic marriage ceremony: the marriage which takes place during Mass – the more usual ceremony – and the marriage outside of Mass, usually celebrated when one of the partners is not a Catholic. In both ceremonies the rite of marriage itself is the same.

The service begins with a hymn and bible reading, followed by a sermon. The priest calls upon the couple to declare that there is no legal impediment to their marriage and then to declare their consent to marriage 'according to the rite of our holy mother the Church'. Each in turn replies, 'I will'.

The bride and groom then join their right hands and make their vows, beginning 'I call upon these persons here present to witness that I . . . do take thee . . . '. The priest then receives their consent saying 'What God has joined together, let no man put asunder'.

The best man usually places the ring (or rings) on a silver salver, where it is blessed by the priest. The bridegroom places it on the bride's finger with the words:

> (Christian name), take this ring as a sign of my love and fidelity. In the name of the Father, and of the son, and of the Holy Ghost.

If the bridegroom is to receive a ring, the bride puts it on his finger, saying the same words. The Bidding Prayers then follow and, if there is no Mass, the couple go to the sacristy with their witnesses to sign the register. If Mass is to follow, the signing of the register may wait until the end of the service.

The Free Church ceremony

The Free Churches vary in their forms of worship but their marriage ceremonies are similar to those of the Church of England.

The service will usually include the procession, the introductory prayers, the declaration that there is no legal impediment to the marriage, the blessing of the ring and the exchange of vows, the blessing and the signing of the register.

Writing your own service

Both inside and outside the Anglican church, there is sometimes an opportunity to include a prayer of your own, specially written to include your own thoughts about marriage. How much you are allowed to contribute to the service depends very much on the minister officiating, but some couples write their own vows, enabling them to make the promises they consider most important. For instance, the words for your special vows might come from the Book of Ruth: 'Wherever you go, I will go. Where you live, I will live. Your people shall be my people and your God my God.'

The Quaker ceremony

The Religious Society of Friends, or Quakers, have their own highly individual form of the marriage ceremony. It includes no procession, no music and no minister. The bride and groom usually sit facing the meeting, with their family and close friends around them. The meeting proceeds along the lines of a regular meeting, with those present sitting in silent worship or rising to speak if they wish.

When the bridal couple feel that the moment is right, they stand and take one another by the hand. The bridegroom says:

> Friends, I take this, my friend . . . to be my wife, promising, through divine assistance, to be unto her a loving and faithful husband so long as we both on earth shall live.

The bride makes a similar promise, changing the appropriate words. There is no set moment for an exchange of rings and though this can be done immediately after the vows, it often waits until the couple sign the register at the end of the meeting.

The Jewish ceremony

The exact form of the ceremony varies between Orthodox and more liberal communities but in most the bridegroom arrives first, accompanied by his father, the bride's father and his best man. When the ceremony is due to begin the groom and his best man under the *chuppah*, a canopy supported by four metal or wooden poles, symbolic of the bridal chamber, while the two father join the bridal procession.

The bride enters on the arm of her father, followed by her bridemaids, the groom's parents and her mother, escorted by a male relative. She stands on the bridegroom's right and both sets of parents join them under the *chuppah*. The procession is often accompanied by singing, with Psalms 80 and 100 being particular favourites.

The rabbi or minister welcomes the couple and gives a short address, followed by betrothal blesings, recited over a cup of wine. The bridegroom places the ring on the bride's right index finger, saying, 'By this ring you are married to me in holiness according to the law of Moses and of Israel.' The ring is considered so important in the marriage ceremony that the bride should wear no other jewellery. She may transfer it to her 'ring' finger later.

The *ketuba*, or marriage document, is then read out. In Orthodox congregations, this will be in Aramic, but Reform congregations usually use Hebrew and both follow by a brief translation. In the Aramic, this includes several clauses designed to ensure that the bride has financial security in case she is divorced or widowed. Next comes the singing or reciting of the 'seven benedictions' and both bride and groom take a sip from a cup of wine as a symbol that in future they will share everything.

The bridegroom then breaks a glass underfoot. This is often said to be a reminder of the destruction of the temple in Jerusalem, but a simpler explanation is that it was an ancient way of frightening away evil spirits: friends often call out '*mazzal tov*' or 'good luck' at this moment. Yet another possibility is that it demonstrates how easily marital happiness can be shattered, unless sufficient care is taken.

The service ends with a priestly blessing and a psalm of praise. The couple sign the register and then retire to a private room together to spend a few minutes alone, as a symbol of their new married status.

At the end of the reception which follows, the seven blessings will be repeated.

Double weddings

When two couples marry in the same ceremony, each couple will have their own best man and bridesmaids. If the brides are sisters, their father may give both of them away and the elder sister will walk first up the aisle and make her vows first. When they are not sisters, then the elder bridegroom and his bride take precedence.

In the procession to the altar, the first bride will be escorted by her father and followed by her attendants, then comes the second bride with her father (or another male member of the family, if they are sisters), followed by her attendants. Both grooms wait at the front of the church, each with his best man. As the procession approaches, the first groom will stand in the centre of the aisle with the second to his right. As their brides join them, the attendants may separate so that those of the first bride stand on the left, those of the second on the right. This may depend on the space available in the church, so careful rehearsal is necessary.

Another possibility, if the brides decide to 'share' bridesmaids, is for them to walk up the aisle side by side without male escorts, followed by their attendants. This would be especially suitable if they were omitting the 'giving away' ceremony from the service.

The ceremony will proceed as usual until the time comes for the couple to make their responses, then each couple will complete each section of the service in their turn.

There are two schools of thought about the procession down the aisle at the end of the ceremony. Each bridal party may be complete in itself, the first bride and groom followed by their attendants and relatives, then the second bride and groom with their attendants. Alternatively the first couple lead, followed by the second couple, then the first best man and bridesmaid, the second best man and chief bridesmaid and the remaining bridesmaids. If the brides are sisters, their mother would walk with the first groom's father, then their father with the first groom's mother.

Relatives or friends of the bride's family may escort the parents of the second groom to complete the procession.

The register office ceremony

The register office ceremony is brief and simple, lasting only ten to fifteen minutes. Whether the bride and groom choose to arrive together or separately, they must make sure they are prompt. On a busy Saturday morning a late arrival may throw out the whole schedule, leaving wedding parties queuing in the street, or may mean that you miss your turn and have to wait until later. Arriving too early can cause problems, too. Register offices have limited waiting room space and it is unfair to crowd the parties ahead of you on the list. Ten minutes ahead is usually about right.

The marriage itself will consist only of what is required by civil law. The Superintendent Registrar begins by reminding the couple of the solemn and binding nature of the vows they are about to undertake. Each must then repeat, 'I do solemnly declare that I know of no legal impediment why I . . . may not be joined in matrimony to . . .'. Then they turn to one another and say in turn: 'I call upon these persons here present to witness that I . . . do take thee . . . to my lawful wedded wife/husband.' The groom can then put the ring on the bride's finger, but there need be no ring, as it has no legal significance. The registrar will then fill in the marriage lines and the bride and groom sign the register.

After the ceremony

Some couples leave the church through a guard of honour. This often happens when either the bride or groom is in the forces and friends form an arch of crossed swords, but guards of honour are not reserved for military weddings. If either of you is interested in sport, you might leave through an arch of cricket bats, hockey sticks or tennis racquets, or there might be an arch made from strings of artificial flowers or ribbon streamers. If an arch seems a little contrived, the guard of honour might be children from the school where the bride or groom teaches or the members of the local amateur operatic company.

If there is no reception, or it is limited to close family and friends and neighbours have come to the service only, the couple and their parents could form a receiving line outside the church, to thank everyone for coming and receive good wishes.

Most minister these days discourage or forbid the throwing of confetti. They might relent if you can promise a couple of helpers with brooms to sweep up afterwards, but even then little coloured bits are likely to lodge in cracks and bed into the grass, so it is better to reserve confetti for later. Rice is a possible alternative, as the birds will do the clearing up, but the grains can be quite painful when thrown by guests with a good sporting aim.

The bridal party, who need to be on hand to greet the guests at the reception, must be allowed to leave first: the bride and groom in the first car and immediately afterwards the bridesmaids, possibly with the bride's parents sharing the car. Next it is the turn of the groom's parents.

The receiving line

The idea of the receiving line is to make sure that every guest is greeted and introduced to both families. The usual arrangement is:

Bride's mother
Bride's father
Groom's mother
Groom's father
Bride
Groom
Chief bridesmaid
Bridesmaids

The best man is not usually included as he should be the last to leave the church and when he does arrive at the reception, he is usually better employed in checking that everything is going to plan.

All sorts of variations are possible in the receiving line. If there is a large number of guests, the formal greeting can go on for so long that the celebrations are held up for half an hour, so it might be better for the attendants to mingle with the guests instead, or for the bride and groom to receive alone. When the hosts named on the wedding invitations were not the bride's parents, then they would normally take the parents' place in the receiving line.

A divorced couple can stand together on the receiving line but if this causes embarrassment, it might be better to dispense with the line altogether or opt for a different arrangement: for instance, bride's mother, groom's father, bride's father, groom's mother.

The receiving line is not the place to catch up on news or reminisce with old friends; a brief welcome on one side, congratulations and good wishes on the other, are quite sufficient. Friends of the groom, and anyone else who has not met the bride's family, should introduce themselves to the bride's mother. Friends of the bride's family will be introduced to the groom's family as they pass down the line.

Some guests may arrive with presents, so it is a good idea to have a small table nearby so that the parcels can be stacked there, to be collected at the end of the day. If you know that a large number of presents will be arriving on the day, you might detail someone to arrange a display around the cake on a side table. No one will expect you to open the presents on the spot; a simple 'Thank-you so much, we shall look forward to opening that later' will be enough acknowledgement for the moment.

The line should stay in place until every guest has been received but that does not mean holding up the entire reception because Uncle Wilf had a puncture on his way from the church. If late-comers are expected, one of the ushers or a young relative might be asked to hover near the door and alert the bridal couple when they arrive, or steer them towards their places at table.

The meal

There should be only a brief gap between the last guests being received and served with drinks and the beginning of the meal, as by then the early arrivals may be becoming restive. If a buffet is to be served, the bridal couple might lead the way to the buffet table to be served first, or the bride's father might rap on the nearest hard surface and ask everyone to help themselves.

For a sit-down meal, the bride's mother usually gives the signal for the bridal party to lead the way and the rest of the guests follow. Large receptions will have a seating plan near the entrance so that everyone will have a good idea where they are sitting, but for a small family party the best man, or perhaps a reliable uncle, should be given the task of ushering everyone towards the right seats. On no account should guests be left wandering round and round the table peering at the names on place cards.

A more dramatic launch to the celebrations can be achieved if the bride and groom make a ceremonial entry when all their guests are seated. They will need to slip away a few minutes before the guests are invited to take their seats and then whoever is acting as toastmaster will knock three times and announce 'Ladies and gentlemen, please stand to greet the bride and groom, Mr and Mrs Willoughby Winters'. Everyone enjoys hearing the bride's married name announced for the first time in this dignified fashion and the ceremonial entry need not be reserved for baronial hall receptions. Even in a church hall or a private house the bride and groom can spend a couple of minutes in another room or a hallway, or even outside if necessary.

Saying grace

If the minister is present, he should be asked to say grace. Otherwise, including or omitting grace is a matter for the family and may depend on their own religious beliefs, but it is in keeping with the spirit of a church wedding.

When everyone is seated the appointed toastmasters should announce 'Ladies and gentlemen, the Reverend Arthur Preach will now say grace.' If the minister is not present, grace might be said by the bride's father, by another member of the wedding party or, if the family feel it more suitable, by one of the guests. The simple, well-known graces may be used:

> For what we are about to receive, may the Lord
> make us truly thankful.

or

> Bless, O Lord, this food to our use and us to thy service.

Other words more suitable to the day may be used and a grace composed by the bridal couple or one of the family will have special significance and make it more likely that guests will take note of the words. Some possibilities are:

> Thank-you, Lord, for this food before us, for the love of our families and for the love of Michael and Jane on their wedding day.

or

> Bless this food, O Lord, as you bless Michael and Jane on this happy day.

Cutting the cake

When the meal is over, usually an hour to an hour and a half after the guests sit down (depending on the number of courses and speed of service), the toastmaster will announce, 'Ladies and gentlemen, may I have your attention please. The bride and groom will now cut the cake.'

To cut the cake, the bride holds the knife in her right hand. The groom's right hand goes over hers, then the bride puts her left hand on top. They need only make the first cut, then the cake will be taken away to be cut into small slices and handed round after the speeches. Sometimes the bride and groom hand round the cake themselves, so that they make sure of having a few words with everyone. If the reception is to continue into the evening, the cake cutting may be reserved until later.

The speeches

Three speeches are usual at a wedding:
1. The toast to the health and happiness of the bride and groom.
2. The response by the bridegroom, who toasts the bridesmaids.
3. The best man replies on behalf of the attendants.
The first speaker is often the bride's father, though he may delegate the task to an old family friend or a favourite uncle who can sing the bride's praises more easily. If both a father and stepfather are

involved in the wedding one might escort her in church and the other speak at the reception.

You may prefer less than three speeches: if the bride and groom have arranged their own wedding, then the groom might thank everyone for coming and the best man might propose the health of the couple. On the other hand, there could be more than three – but remember that guests will become restless if they go on too long. An additional speech might come from the groom's father, thanking the bride's family for all their hard work and welcoming his new daughter-in-law into the family. If you have someone renowned for after-dinner speeches among the guests you might ask him, or her, to propose one of the toasts or to make an extra speech.

If there are no bridesmaids, the best man need not speak at all. The groom could toast the bride and she could reply. The idea that only men speak at weddings dies hard, but there is no reason why the bride cannot speak instead of her husband, or the mother of the bride propose the first toast, especially if she is hosting the wedding alone. If a bridesmaid is a more confident speaker than the best man, she might respond to the groom's toast. If you do choose an unconventional arrangement of speakers, make sure everyone is consulted and that they understand your reasons, so that no feelings are hurt. (See Chapter 9, p.111, for content of speeches.)

Once all the speeches are over, the best man usually reads out any telemessages, once he has made sure they are suitable for family ears. At Jewish weddings, a final toast to 'Her Majesty the Queen' is customary.

The evening reception

If the reception is to go on into the evening, it is not necessary for guests to stay until the bride and groom have left but they should say their goodbyes quickly and quietly to avoid disrupting the proceedings.

When dancing is included, the bride and groom should be the first on the floor, whether announced or unannounced. They should dance alone for the first couple of minutes, then the bride's father and the groom's mother take the floor, then the groom's father and the bride's mother, followed by the best man and the chief bridesmaid. As ushers and bridesmaids join them on the floor, they should encourage other guests to join in, as everyone may be reluctant to make the first move.

The cake cutting may take place at any time during the evening but be careful not to leave it too late, or quite a number of the older guests may have left. The ceremony should be announced, just as it would have been at the meal table, or half the guests may miss it.

The informal reception

Degrees of informality vary: you might still want to receive guests at the door, cut the cake at an appointed time, have all the usual speeches and drive off afterwards with all your friends and relatives waving you goodbye, or you might prefer simply to ply your friends with food and drink and forget the rest.

At the sort of reception where guests are likely to spread out all around the house and garden, it might be a good idea to tell everyone where and when you plan to cut the cake, then send some of the younger members of the family to collect in the stragglers at the appointed time.

The more informal the reception, the shorter the speeches will probably be. You may plan cake cutting without any speeches but remember that *someone* is likely to shout out 'Speech, speech!' so either the groom or best man should be ready to say a few words if pressed – even if it is only 'Thank-you all for coming and please go on having a good time.'

The double reception

If all the parents and attendants are included in the receiving line it will be impossibly long. The usual solution is to include only the hosts – the bride's parents if the girls are sisters, otherwise both host couples and the brides and grooms. The onus will be on the guests to introduce themselves by name, perhaps adding 'John's school-friend' or 'Robert's uncle'.

Having two sets of speeches is likely to lead to repetition and boredom, so it is usual for one person to propose the toast to both couples and one best man to speak. You might leave the two best men to sort that out for themselves and decide which of them is the better speaker, but if that is likely to lead to problems, the best man assisting the senior bridegroom (i.e. the best man to the groom who led the bridal procession) should be asked to do the job. If the bridegrooms are brothers one might speak for both but more usually both bridegrooms speak – preferably briefly – and the second proposes the toast to the bridesmaids.

Going away

After a sit-down meal, once the speeches are over and the cake eaten, the couple should circulate among their guests, trying to make sure they have a word with everyone but not settling in for a long chat anywhere. Then they will retire to change into their going-away clothes.

Last-minute goodbyes and thank-yous to parents should be kept short as by now everyone will be milling about waiting for the departure. Tradition says that the bride should throw her bouquet into the waiting crowd and that the girl who catches it will be the next to be married.

You will be lucky to escape the tail of tin cans or old shoes on the back of the car or lipstick messages on the windscren, so it is a good idea to take along a roll of kitchen paper and some scissors so that you can stop in the nearest lay-by and remove the evidence. If this sort of thing really bothers you, it would be better to have a trustworthy friend leave your car a mile away and leave the reception in a car hire, or have the friend drive you.

Wedding announcements

A newspaper announcement of the wedding will probably read simply:

> BROWN:GREEN – On 10 September at St Ethelred's Parish Church, Meltington, Jeremy Woodhouse Brown to Arabella, daughter of Col. and Mrs Frederick Green of Meltington, West Midlands

If the couple have many relatives and friends living abroad, or were married quietly and quickly without telling everyone, they might send out printed announcements after the event. These might be worded formally:

> Miss Arabella Green and Mr Jeremy Brown beg to announce that they were married quietly at St Ethelred's Parish Church, Meltington on 10 September.

or informally:

> Arabella and Peter are delighted to tell you that they were married at Meltington Register Office on 10 September and hope that you will visit soon at 35 Trumpton Road, Meltington.

Wedding day superstitions

All over the world, sunshine on the day is supposed to bring good luck and the saying 'Happy is the bride the sun shines on' has its counterpart in many languages. It might be comforting to some brides to know that snow is just as good an omen. In America there is a longstanding belief that the weather pattern of the wedding day forecasts the outlook for married life. If the morning is fine and the afternoon stormy, the couple's new-found happiness will not last long. If the day starts wet and clears as it goes along, the bride and groom will need some patience before their life together runs smoothly.

Most couples still follow the old superstition that it is unlucky to see one another on the wedding morning, before they meet for the ceremony. The bride can help good fortune along by feeding her cat before she leaves for the ceremony (that means no rain for the rest of the day) and putting a penny in her shoe (carrying a coin ensure prosperous days ahead). On the other hand, she must be very careful not to break anything, for fear of bringing bad luck to the marriage, and she must never, never cry on her wedding day. Even tears of joy mean tears of sorrow for all the years to come.

Good omens seen by the bride on the way to the wedding include a lamb, a spider, a toad, a black cat and a grey horse in a field. On the other hand a pig crossing her path is bad news and a nun is not much better! The bridal car with its white ribbons should never be turned within sight of the bride or groom, or they will suffer a 'reverse' of fortune. Drivers of specialist hired cars usually keep this in mind, even today.

The bridegroom has little to worry about, though he should never turn back once he has left the house on his way to the ceremony. The best man can help the couple's good fortune by giving an odd sum of money when he pays the church fees in the vestry.

Brides who want children should be sure to cut the first slice of cake, with the groom's help, and putting away a crumb for safe keeping means that her husband will always be faithful. The bride and groom should share the first piece of cake, breaking off small pieces and sharing them. This custom is echoed in many cultures, as a symbol of the happy sharing of their life ahead. Moslem couples bite into the same sweetmeat and in the Eastern Orthodox church, each partner drinks three times from a cup of wine.

Wedding anniversaries

Most families mark only silver, golden and diamond weddings with special celebrations and, perhaps, gifts to match the anniversary but if you want to mark each anniversary in an appropriate way, the list runs as follows:

1st anniversary	cotton	13th	lace
2nd	paper	14th	ivory
3rd	leather or straw	15th	crystal
4th	silk	20th	china
5th	wood	25th	silver
6th	iron	30th	pearl
7th	wool	35th	coral
8th	bronze	40th	ruby
9th	pottery	45th	sapphire
10th	tin	50th	gold
11th	steel	55th	emerald
12th	linen	60th and 75th	diamond

9

The Speeches

Weddings mean that people who would normally never dream of addressing a public meeting find themselves standing before fifty or a hundred people, making the first speech of their lives. At a small family party a few off-the-cuff remarks may be all that is needed but at a formal wedding this is not enough. It is an important occasions and speakers owe it to the bridal couple and their families to give time and thought to the preparation of the speech.

This does not mean that anyone expects you to blossom into an expert public speaker overnight. The only essentials are to be brief and relevant, to avoid embarrassing anyone and to give your sincere good wishes to the members of the wedding.

Preparation

Relying on the inspiration of the moment is not for amateurs; inspiration probably will not come and you will find yourself lamely repeating what the previous speaker has said. Sitting down on the wedding eve to write the whole thing from scratch seldom brings good results either. Instead, jot down any ideas you have over the weeks before the wedding, then when you come to plan your speech you can polish and prune, select the most appropriate phrases and discard any remarks that are not so funny on reflection.

Decide what you need to say and what you want to say, then fill out the bare bones with a reminiscence, a joke or an anecdote. Resist the temptation to include *several* reminiscences or anecdotes. A good speech should have a beginning, a middle and an end, rather than stringing together a list of random remarks. Try to begin on a postive, happy note and never start by apologizing for being such a poor speaker, or everyone will expect the worst.

Wedding speeches should always be personal, rather than sounding as though they could have been delivered at any one of a hundred weddings. It may be possible to include an anecdote from the childhood of the bride or groom (but avoid anything that will make them squirm), references to the way the couple met or the interests they have in common.

Tailor your speech to your audience. A gathering of friends and colleagues will enjoy a light-hearted, joky speech; a family wedding with a good proportion of grandparents, great-aunts and elderly uncles will probably prefer more sentiment and less flippancy. Whatever the makeup of the gathering there should be no *risqué* stories or blue jokes – get them all over at the stag night and forget about them! Find out in advance if there are any family members who deserve a special mention: for instance, the groom's Aunt Miriam who has travelled 5000 miles to see him married. If there are relatives on either side who do not speak English, it is courteous to include a sentence or so in their language – and it guarantees you a round of applause. Write down what you want to say and ask someone to record the translation on tape. You can then listen to it and learn it by heart or take the wise precaution of writing it down phonetically, just as it sounds to you, so that you can use it as a memory prompt on the day.

Consider how you are going to refer to anyone named in your speech: do you call the groom's parents by their first names or something more formal, or will you simply refer to 'Michael's parents'? If you are referring to the bridesmaids, make sure you know their names. It may sound simple but if they are strangers to you, it is easy to forget in the heat of the moment. Never assume that you can call them by a nickname – Maggie for Margaret or Sam for Samantha – just because you have heard the bride doing so. If in doubt, ask them what they prefer to be called in advance.

Avoid clichés and old chestnuts like 'embarking on the sea of life', 'may all their troubles be little ones' or 'unaccustomed as I am to public speaking' – unless you are a well-known television presenter, in which case it should ensure a laugh. Though wedding speeches normally extol the virtues of the bride and groom, the bridesmaids or whoever is being toasted at the time, fulsome flattery can be embarrassing and it is wiser to avoid superlatives and

112

any hint of gush. Never tell patent untruths, like calling the bridesmaids beautiful if it is obvious to everyone that they are rather plain. It makes your whole speech sound insincere and may even cause a few titters. Choose other complimentary adjectives like charming or delightful instead.

Remembering the speech

If you read your speech it will be hard to sound natural, you will be inclined to look downwards and your rustling papers may distract your audience. On the other hand, if you learn it off by heart something may put you off in the middle and cause you to dry up completely.

There are several middle ways which will help you to keep control of the situation. Many public speakers recommend writing out the speech on a series of postcards, one paragraph to each card, written in large print with the main points underlined. Then you can deliver the speech partly from memory, partly with the prompting of the cards. If you use this method, be sure to number the cards in large letters, so that if you lose your place, you can quickly put things right.

If you are a little more confident of your memory, edit your speech down to a series of 'bullets', a list of the main points in your speech and key words from any joke or anecdote you plan to include and list them clearly on a card you can hold in your hand. This will make sure you leave nothing out and is especially suitable if you are confident enough to speak without planning every single word in advance. However, it is not a substitute for forward thinking and you should still know exactly what you want to say and what you want to leave out.

Consider the options, but if you feel unsure of yourself, worry that you will drop all the postcards or be unable to remember a single word to go with your bullets, then settle for reading your speech. Use heavy paper so that it rustles as little as possible and underline all the main points so that, if your memory holds up better than you had hoped on the day, you can just use it as backup.

Rehearsing the speech

It is very important to rehearse your speech so that it becomes familiar without having to learn it parrot-fashion. You can also time it to make sure it is not too long: three minutes is often quite long enough and five minutes is about the maximum, unless the speaker is exceptionally polished and witty.

Stand up when you rehearse so that you make sure you can read the notes that you have prepared. Ordinary handwriting is very difficult to read under these circumstances, so have your notes typewritten or write them in large letters with a felt-tipped pen. Many speakers advise rehearsing in front of a mirror so that you practise keeping your head up and catch any irritating mannerisms like fiddling with your glasses or chinking the change in your pocket.

A tape recorder can be useful to show you if you are inclining to say 'you know' or 'I mean' in every second sentence or punctuate the whole thing with 'ums' and 'ers'. Try to vary the pace and emphasis of your voice; the most interesting speech in the world will bore the listeners if it is delivered all on one note. Best of all is to ask a friend to 'hear' you, then you can gauge how much time you should allow for 'audience reaction'.

Humour

Using humour in a speech is far more adventurous than being serious, especially with an audience that may range in age from three to ninety-three. When deciding on the content of your speech, try not to feel that you *must* be funny. If you have to strain to do it, then opt for brief sincerity instead. Make an honest assessment of your ability to tell funny stories: do you tend to lose yourself in the middle, forget the punchline or dissolve into helpless laughter halfway through? If so, forget about them.

A witty one-liner or a well-chosen quotation is safer than a joke but if you do include a joke (*never* plan a string of jokes for a wedding speech) make sure that it is short and punchy and if possible, turn it into a personal anecdote. 'That reminds me of the one about the wedding where the bridegroom . . . ' kills your story before you start; you will find your audience far more receptive if you turn it round to say 'At the last wedding I went to the bridegroom . . . ' Steer clear of religious or ethnic jokes and any dated humour about the little woman slaving over a hot stove for her man.

Be ready with a few 'off the cuff' remarks that you might be able to use on the day, as these often raise a bigger laugh than funny stories. If a police siren sounds in the street outside, you might say, 'One last word before they take me away' or ask a waiter hurrying to and fro in the background 'Are you on a sponsored walk?' or, if someone drops a tray, 'Save the applause until the end, please.' Such comments may not look particularly funny in cold print but delivered on the spur of the moment, everyone will be delighted with your quick-wittedness.

Make sure that you pause for laughter, rather than wasting the next sentence by carrying on through it, but if your remark raises smiles rather than laughs, be ready to go straight on.

Delivery

When you rise to your feet, pause long enough to register your presence but not long enough to wonder why you are standing there dumbstruck. Take a deep breath and speak at a comfortable pace, rather than gabbling as though you are anxious to get the whole thing over as quickly as possible. Concentrate on what you are saying and pay as much attention to the end of the sentence as to the beginning. Never try to alter your natural voice to sound more impressive; it is likely to revert to normal in the middle and cause unplanned laughter.

After all the preparation you want to be sure that everyone can hear you, so speak loudly enough for your voice to reach the back of the room without bellowing. It may be helpful to arrange for a signal from someone at the farthest corner to indicate whether or not they can hear you clearly. If you are using a microphone, try not to stand so near that it picks up every breath, or so far away that you might as well not be using it, and avoid swaying to and fro so that you fade in and out. If the microphone gives trouble, emitting high pitched whines or refusing to adjust to the right level, push it aside and do without it. Stopping to put things right will spoil the whole effect of a short speech.

Remember that you are speaking to an appreciative audience, happy and mellow and ready to laugh and applaud in all the right places, but if you find the sea of expectant faces unnerving, focus on the face of your wife or girlfriend or mother at the beginning and then, as her encouraging expression gives you confidence, you can take in the rest of the room. Otherwise, just begin with a broad smile. Everyone will smile back and the benevolent atmosphere will do wonders for your shaky nerves.

Stag party speeches

This is the time for speakers to get all the bawdy jokes out of their system. The tradition is for the best man to insult the bridegroom and make as much fun of the institution of marriage as possible while the bridegroom tries to be even more insulting in return. Usually the speakers can rely on alcohol to blunt their listeners' critical faculties.

The speech from a bachelor best man might begin:

> Gentlemen – welcome to the wake. We are gathered here tonight to mourn the memory of another good man gone, gone to answer the call of the dishwasher and the deep freeze. We, the free, must promise to pour an extra gin and tonic to his memory whenever two or more are gathered together.
>
> Just imagine an educated, cultured girl like Anna picking John! I felt it was my duty to warn her that he's the sort of man who thinks he can save time by stopping his watch. When he went to buy his wedding tie there was a power failure and he was stuck on Harrods' (or name a local store) escalator for twenty minutes. But she wouldn't listen and I couldn't persuade her that there was a clever, witty, handsome substitute on hand if she changed her mind.
>
> So this is our last chance to give John good advice as he walks innocently into the jaws of matrimony. He needs to remember that marriage is just like any other job; you get on much better if you like the boss. And if an argument breaks out, there's one way a husband can always get the last word – apologize!

If the best man is married, he might include:

> I remember my wedding day. The mother-in-law was there with the handcuffs; as she walked down the aisle they were clanking against her jackboots. The bride's little brother George gave her away – he told me who she'd been to Brighton with the weekend before.
>
> I couldn't fancy her at first – I didn't know women went to bed in shaving cream. I thought there was something wrong with me. I went to the doctor and told him that the first time I made love to my wife I felt miserably hot; the second I felt bitterly cold. He couldn't find anything wrong so he called in the wife and asked her about. She rolled about laughing. She told him the first time was in July and the second time was in December.

Either of the speeches might end:

> So let's drink to John and pass the cigars as we remember Rudyard Kipling's immortal words: 'A woman is only a woman. But a good cigar is a smoke.'

The bridegroom's reply could include:

> Peter Ustinov once said that friends aren't necessarily the people you like best, they are merely the people who got there first. On nights like this, I see his point.
>
> The trouble with bachelors is that they think they are things of beauty when they are really boys forever. Tony throws these insults about to cover up his envy. He's never had much success with women. There was the time when we saw one lovely girl after another going into his office, but that was only because he had stuck a notice saying 'Ladies' on the door. When they took his notice away, he wrote to a Lonely Hearts club but they wrote back saying that they weren't *that* lonely!

Wedding toast to the bride and groom

The speaker needs to compliment the bride and groom; he might talk about the joy of knowing the bride throughout her life and the pleasure of getting to know the bridegroom, perhaps mentioning how much the bride and groom have in common and commenting on their good fortune in finding one another.

The speech by an uncle or godfather might run like this:

> I am pleased and honoured to be asked to propose this toast. I have known Anna for most of her life – all but twenty-four hours of it, to be exact – and, as a devoted uncle, I was ready to be critical of any man who wanted to marry her. But as soon as I was introduced to John, I recognized him as a man of taste and discernment – after all, look at the girl he chose.
>
> I am confident that John and Anna have all the qualities they need to build a strong and successful marriage. They both have the sense of humour to help them through difficult patches, the warmth and sympathy to support one another when things go wrong and the courage and determination essential to make sure thing go right.
>
> Let me ask you to raise your glasses and drink to the health and happiness of the bride and groom.

A friend, asked to propose the toast at a small, informal wedding party, could say:

> I am very honoured, as I am sure you are, to be one of the few close friends invited to share this day with John and Anna. We all know them as warm-hearted, generous (or clever, talented; or lively, fun-loving) people, so they can only bring out the best in one another and I am certain that theirs will be a long and happy marriage. They certainly deserve the best, so let's raise out glasses and drink to Anna and John.

Toast to the bridesmaids

The bridegroom, replying on behalf of himself and his wife, is mainly concerned with thanking everyone. No one expects him to be wildly funny, in fact he should show that he is conscious of the meaning of the occasion and its importance to him. His speech mainly consists of thanking everyone: the previous speaker, the bride's parents and probably his parents as well, the guests for their presence and their presents. Finally he thanks the attendants for their help and support and proposes the health of the bridesmaids. He might speak as follows:

> My wife and I (pause for applause) thank you for your good wishes. I can't imagine a happier way to start married life than with our family and friends around us. By coming here today you have helped to make this a wonderful day for us and by your magnificent response to our appeal you have helped to make our new home a very attractive and comfortable place, so we hope you will visit us there before too long.
>
> Our thanks must go to our parents, of course, for making the whole thing possible. We have both grown up knowing the real meaning of marriage because of their example. I am especially grateful to my new parents-in-law for giving us this lovely wedding – and, even more, for producing a daughter like Anna!
>
> Now, before I sit down, I know you would like to join me in thanking the charming young ladies who have added so much to the occasion, so please join me in drinking a toast to the bridesmaids.

Of course, speeches need to be adjusted to all sorts of different family circumstances. If, for instance, the bride's parents are absent for some reason and the groom's parents have taken on the lion's share of arranging or paying for the wedding, he might say:

> I can see that you are all enjoying this lovely party arranged by Anna, aided and abetted by my father and mother, who can't be kept away from any party. When I said this was the bride's show, they said they had always wanted a girl anyway and weren't going to be done out of their fun because I had the bad taste to turn out to be a boy. Could I help it? So Anna and I want to thank them for all they have done for us – we know how lucky we are to have them around.

The best man's reply

If he wants to take no risks, all the best man need do is say what an honour and pleasure it has been to perform his wedding tasks and thank the bridegroom, on the bridesmaids' behalf, for his good wishes. In practice, his speech is usually an excuse for a few witticisms about marriage or weddings and some teasing of the bridegroom. Needless to say, any jokes at the expense of the bride or her mother would be disastrously out of place. His speech might sound like this:

When I accepted the role of best man at this wedding, I was full of foreboding. I knew that my duties would be many and onerous. I would be the one to soothe the bridegroom's shattered nerves and prevent any wedding day panic. I would have to help him dress, as he would obviously be incapable of managing alone, and guide his faltering footsteps to the church door. In fact, when I arrived and pressed the doorbell with a shaking hand, he was already dressed and keen to set off – a mere two hours before the ceremony was due to begin. I never saw a man less eager to make a run for it at the last moment.

I filled in the time by trying to find out how John persuaded such a lovely girl to marry him. Of course, he has plenty of good qualities. He's always been modest – but then, he has plenty to be modest about. He doesn't know the meaning of egotism. Well, he doesn't know the meaning of lots of other words either! I know that he will remember the most important marriage maxim: 'Nothing makes a good wife like a good husband.' And as for Anna, I'm sure she knows that a wife should share everything with her husband – including the housework.

I've discovered today why every wedding needs bridesmaids. It's because an unfortunate bachelor like me is likely to despair once the bride has been snapped up. The delightful bridesmaids are there to restore his faith and hope. So my final wedding duty is a real pleasure; it is to thank the groom on the bridesmaids' behalf for his kind words and to say how much we all share the happiness of John and Anna on their special day.

Material for speeches

Books of quotations and one-liners are a good source of material for speeches and can be found on the shelves of any public library. The following quotations and anecdotes may help to spark off your own ideas.

Quotations
Speech is great but silence is greater. (Carlyle)

It usually takes me more than three weeks to prepare a good impromptu speech. (Mark Twain)

A husband should tell his wife everything he thinks she will find out. (Thomas R. Dewar)

Don't give a woman advice. One should never give a woman anything she can't wear in the evening. (Oscar Wilde)

Love doesn't make the world go round. Love is what makes the ride worthwhile. (Franklin P. Jones)

Never go to bed mad. Stay up and fight. (Phyllis Diller)

Marriage is popular because it combines the maximum of temptation with the maximum of opportunity. (George Bernard Shaw)

Married couples resemble a pair of scissors, often moving in opposite directions, yet always punishing anyone who comes between them. (Sydney Smith)

Quick quips
He (the bridegroom) is a very balanced chap – he's got a chip on each shoulder.

Once married you have half the grief, double the joy – and treble the expenses.

We all know that women have genuine equality these days. I only said so to my sister this morning as she was cleaning my shoes.

Just a word of advice to John. If your wife doesn't treat you as she should – be thankful!

When John started his own business, he had nothing but his own drive and intelligence. You can't start smaller than that.

This is indeed a day to remember. The day that John bought the drinks.

There's no doubt that men have better taste than women. After all, John chose Anna – but Anna chose John.

Every time I get up to speak some idiot begins talking.

May bad luck follow you all your life – and never catch up with you.
I can't stand namedroppers. I was only saying so to Margaret
Thatcher the other day.

John is the most independent salesman I know – he doesn't take
orders from anyone.

Jokes and anecdotes

Thank goodness I'm not like the father forced into a speech at his
daughter's wedding who ended up saying, 'I feel I should say a few
complimentary words about Marmaduke but I'm like a dog in a
street full of lampposts – short of material and not a leg to stand on.'
(Best used at an informal wedding with plenty of young friends in
the audience.)

The last time I spoke at a wedding a man fell asleep. When I asked
one of the pageboys to wake him up, the horrible child said, '*You*
wake him up. You were the one who put him to sleep.'

When John asked Harold (name the bride's father) if he could
marry Anna, Harold asked him if he reckoned he could support a
family. John told him he was only thinking of supporting Anna. The
rest of us would have to look after ourselves. (Suitable if the first
toast is proposed by a relative other than the bride's father.)

The last wedding I went to was so posh, it made your teeth ache.
The man next to me was going on about his titled ancestors. I said,
'You'll be telling me next your ancestors sailed with Noah in the
ark.' He looked down a very long nose: 'Great heavens no. My
people had their own boat.'

I was at a wedding the other week where they had one of these
present displays. In pride of place was a fat cheque from the bride's
father. Then along came a bloke, picks up the cheque and falls
about laughing. When I asked the bride who was the ill-mannered
lout, she said, 'Daddy's bank manager.' (More suitable at a wedding without a present display.)

One of my uncles celebrated his golden wedding last week and I
asked him how he had managed to stay happily married for so long.
He said he let his wife take all the minor decisions and took all the

big decisions himself. She decided on how many children to have, which house to buy, how much money they needed to live on. She left it to him to decide whether to ban the bomb, bring back hanging or outlaw trade unions.

10

Wedding Countdown and Wedding Day Diary

When you become engaged
○ Choose the date.
○ Arrange newspaper announcement.
○ Decide what sort of wedding you want: church or register office, formal or informal, large or small.
○ Decide what sort of honeymoon you are having: a weekend away, a holiday abroad, a couple of weeks decorating your new home.

As soon as the date is decided
○ For a church wedding, fix the date and time with the minister.
○ For a register office wedding, give notice to the registrar (up to three months before the day).
○ Book the reception and caterers – just the date and time at this stage; details can wait until later.
○ Self-caterers may need to book a hall or the hire of a marquee.
○ Book transport to the church, photographs, someone to video the proceedings.
○ Choose the best man, bridesmaids, attendants and ushers and check that the date is convenient for them.
○ Make the travel arrangements for your honeymoon and order a new passport, if necessary.

During the next few weeks
○ Decide on numbers for the reception and draw up your guest list.
○ Order your wedding stationery: plan wording of invitations and order of service.
○ Begin planning your wedding outfits. Discuss styles and colours

with the bridesmaids. Make arrangements for hiring or having them made.
○ Order the cake or make it yourself, with plenty of time to mature.

Eight weeks before the wedding
○ Arrange for the banns to be called – in two parishes if you live in different areas.
○ Check final details of the service, bellringing and choir with the minister. Check on fees involved.
○ If necessary, arrange a church rehearsal.
○ Order the flowers for bride's and bridesmaids' bouquets, buttonholes, church and reception.
○ See caterers to plan menu in detail.
○ Self-caterers should plan menus, enlist enough helpers beforehand and for the day itself and check on supplies of crockery, cutlery and linen.
○ Shop for going-away outfits.
○ Plan your pre-wedding parties.
○ Discuss both mothers' outfits with them to prevent any embarrassing clash.
○ Arrange hire of morning suits, if necessary.
○ Buy wedding rings.

Six weeks before
○ Send out invitations
○ Make present list and be ready to send it to anyone who asks for it.
○ Choose accessories for bride and bridesmaids.
○ Choose presents for your attendants.
○ Book bride's hair appointments for the wedding day and for a week beforehand, to try out hairstyle and headdress.

Four weeks before
○ Confirm orders with caterers, photographers, car hire firm, florist.
○ Self-caterers should order wine and arrange loan of glasses, also list food supplies needed.
○ Check that all your outfits are complete and have a 'dress rehearsal' in case any last-minute alterations are necessary.

○ Make arrangements for any guests who need overnight accommodation.

○ If the bride is changing her name, inform bank, building society, insurance firms, etc.

○ Arrange for newspaper wedding announcement.

○ Check all travel arrangements.

Two weeks before

○ Let the caterers know the final numbers of guests.

○ Make seating plan for the reception and write out place cards.

○ Self-caterers should buy in all non-perishables and order perishables, confirm supplies of china and cutlery, arrange for as much food as possible to be made ahead.

○ Write as many thank-you notes for presents as possible.

○ Make sure all the helpers are clear about their duties.

The final week

○ Attend wedding rehearsal, if arranged.

○ 'Rehearse' wedding day hairstyles and makeup.

○ Self-caterers should check on supplies of food, wine, etc.

○ Plan present display, if any.

○ Confirm order for flowers and time of delivery.

The day before

○ Make sure all your clothes are in the right place and nothing is missing.

○ Pack for the honeymoon.

○ Self-caterers should check all last-minute preparations, lay buffet tables and arrange flowers if necessary.

○ Make up an emergency kit with needle, cotton, tissues, make-up for retouching, and make sure that the bride's mother or a reliable friend keeps it handy.

The wedding morning

○ Keep to your timetable for personal grooming.

○ Transfer your engagement ring to the right hand.

○ When the flowers arrive put them in a cool place; if they are late, ring the florist immediately.

○ Self-caterers should put the finishing touches to food but be sure catering preparations are finished at least an hour before the bridal

party is due to leave for the ceremony.
o Check that the best man has the ring in a safe place.
o Arrive at church or register office on schedule.

Wedding day timetable

The more elaborate the wedding, the more necessary it will be to keep to a timetable. If one part of the celebration runs twenty minutes late, the smooth running of the whole day will be affected. Below is a suggested timetable for a bride and groom planning to leave on honeymoon after a daytime reception. It can be adapted to fit the couple's individual plan of the day.

Before the service
45 minutes before service time: the ushers arrive.
30 minutes before: bellringing begins and the organist starts to play.
20 minutes before: the groom and best man arrive.
15 minutes before: the bridesmaids arrive.
10 minutes before: the bride's mother arrives (unless she has travelled with the bridesmaids).
3–5 minutes before: the bride arrives, allowing time for photographs and last-minute rearrangement of her gown and veil
On time: the bridal procession begins.

After the service
Immediately after the service ends: formal photographs are taken outside.
20 minutes after: the bride and groom leave for the reception.
30 minutes after: the bride and groom arrive at the reception venue and form the receiving line.

At the reception
After 20 minutes spent receiving guests: the signal for guests to take their place at table is given.
After 1–1 ½ hours allowed for the meal: the bride and groom cut the cake.
After 5 minutes for the cake cutting: the toasts and speeches begin.
After 15–20 minutes of speeches: the bride and groom go round the tables for a few words with each guest.

After 15 minutes spent chatting with the guests: the bride and groom leave the reception to change.
After 30 minutes for changing into going-away clothes: the bride and groom say their goodbyes.